T0267226

SCOTLAND
THE
HOW?

THE HOWS AND WHYS OF
SCOTTISH HISTORY
795–1822

SCOTLAND THE HOW?

THE HOWS AND WHYS OF SCOTTISH HISTORY 795–1822

JOHN AND NOREEN HAMILTON

In memory of John Hamilton
1958 – 2022

First published 2022

The History Press
97 St George's Place, Cheltenham,
Gloucestershire, GL50 3QB
www.thehistorypress.co.uk

British Library Cataloguing in Publication Data.
A catalogue record for this book is available from the British Library.

isbn 978 1 80399 045 3

Typesetting and origination by The History Press
Printed and bound in Great Britain by TJ Books Limited, Padstow, Cornwall.

Trees for LYfe

CONTENTS

STARTING THOUGHTS

Scotland is a middle-sized European country (twenty-third out of fifty for population). It is situated on the north-west periphery. Yet it has a huge presence. The Scottish brand identity is recognised across the world. It punches above its weight.

The big question is HOW? And that includes the West of Scotland use of 'HOW': as comedian Kevin Bridges puts it, 'You do not ponder WHY? You demand HOW?'

HOW DID SCOTLAND GET TO BE THE WAY IT IS?

The Hows and Whys

This is what this book sets out to explain. As the Romans retreated, Britain collapsed into what became known as the Dark Ages. It was out of this period that Alba and then Scotland would emerge. The thrust of this book is to tell the story of how north Britain changed from a bunch of warring nations into a country we would recognise as Scotland today. Roughly the thousand years between AD 800 and 1800 or more precisely – AD 795 to 1822.

Scotland the How? is about taking all the disjointed bits of history and joining them up – how is one thing connected to the other?

How is Scotland a 'Historical Nation'?

Philosopher David Hume described Scots as 'the historical nation'.

Scotland has HISTORY, lots of it. We sell it well! It is a major plank of the strategy for attracting tourists.

Visitors to Scotland will find thousands of historic sites, each plying their wares. You can visit castles and read the interpretation boards, which will describe, on different panels, how this venue was important in the ninth or twelfth or seventeenth century. If you are lucky you will get a real human guide who can answer your questions.

For natives, the 'Scottish history' slopped out to generations of Scottish school children was utterly woeful; mostly they had to learn, parrot-like, lists of English monarchs. Scottish characters and events cropped up randomly with no connecting thread. Yet if you stand anywhere in Scotland you can't throw a Mars Bar in any direction without hitting some story from the past!

If you visit Edinburgh's Old Town (no other city wears its history heart on its sleeve more flagrantly than Edinburgh) you will find the Royal Mile with a castle at one end and a palace at the other (and close by the new Scottish Parliament). Along its length you will find 100,000 yards of tartan, you will find the High Kirk of Scotland, you will find the Scottish Parliament, which was abandoned in 1707, you will find a 100,000 images of the Jacobite rebel Bonnie Prince Charlie, you will find the Mercat Cross where many honest and dishonest people had their heads violently removed from their bodies.

Down in the Grassmarket you will find a memorial to the Covenanting martyrs and, nearby, the Covenanters graveyard and a quaint story about a loyal dog.

You will find statues of Robert the Bruce and William Wallace and Charles II (who had more to do with Scotland's story than you might think). (There are quite a few nineteenth- and twentieth-century monuments, but they are for another volume.)

But where is the overwhelming monument that ties Scottish history together? There is a stunning memorial on Princes Street, but this is dedicated to a fiction writer. We'll come to him.

Joining the dots

There is plenty of information: *Scotland the How?* is all about joining the dots.

This book is a sprint through a thousand years of history. It only skims the surface. For every character and every event mentioned there is a much deeper and wider story. They are all there to be discovered.

There are thousands of books each telling a more complete story about any aspect, and more produced every year. Archive sites on the internet mean we can read books long out of print that could previously only be viewed in the best libraries. The internet itself is filled with documentaries and commentaries. It is easy to find papers and lectures by real historians. The best thing about the internet is that anyone can say what they want; the worst thing about the internet is that anyone can say what they want. Proceed with caution but proceed nonetheless!

ABOUT HISTORY

When it comes to history DONT BELIEVE A WORD!
All history is written by somebody. Each writer has a limited amount of information. Even if you were actually at an event, your impressions may be very different from the person who was standing beside you. As humans we are very good at fooling ourselves, we remember selectively and rewrite our own stories. That's supposing we are trying to be honest.

Every writer has an agenda. What they write will inevitably be coloured by their own preconceptions and prejudices. There is also a very distinct possibility that they are deliberately trying to deceive. It is extremely common for any generation or any new regime to overwrite the past to show themselves in the best possible light. Sorting the lies and damn lies from the merely misinformed is quite a task.

And things CHANGE
For archaeologists any excavation has the potential to turn up a find that turns previous thinking on its head. For example, twenty-first-century explorations on Orkney have revealed a previously

unknown temple complex of a sophistication never before imagined. Impressions of the Neolithic across Britain will need to be reviewed.

For historians a newly discovered document may reveal (once you have discounted forgery) that someone or other was guilty or was innocent. The story has to change.

And fashions CHANGE
Attitudes and opinions, particularly in regards to issues such as race and gender, which were taken as mainstream a century ago would be unthinkable today.

And historians CHANGE THEIR MINDS
If history was complete, historians would be out of a job. Each generation and each individual is bound to re-examine and re-interpret what was written before.

And people and even nations FORGET!
Scotland's great Statement of the Nation, the Declaration of Arbroath, dismisses the heritage of most of Scotland's own population in a sentence.

There is no TRUE version – THERE ARE ONLY STORIES
So how can we come to an understanding of the past? The answer is to read ALL the stories, or at least more than one. Sometimes an account that is patently partisan can be helpful: at least you know what the bias is to start.

ABOUT THIS BOOK

When it comes to 'don't believe a word', the authors happily include these words. This book contains no original research. It is cobbled together from commonly available books and resources, though always from more than one source.

We did not set out with any particular point to prove or axe to grind but doubtless prejudices and opinions are in there. We are not trained historians. We are storytellers and our object throughout has been to tell the story as clearly and simply as we can.

L.R.N. Gray coined the maxim 'add lightness and simplificate'. He was talking about designing aircraft but it applies to just about any design task. We have borne it in mind.

In teaching oral storytelling we always urge tellers to strip the story down to its basics. We have tried to keep the number of characters to a minimum, but nothing happens in a vacuum. For every person mentioned there is a whole cast of characters making things happen – to them we apologise.

The book is largely about kings and the occasional queen. For the period from the Dark Ages to the eighteenth century it really was a 'game of thrones'. A king might spend a great deal of effort (and lives) trying to achieve and maintain his crown. The whole thrust of the politics of the nation revolved around him.

We love social histories that try to reconstruct the lives of men and women, but that is not this book. In the earlier centuries there is very little information about the lives of common folk. We know most about the clergy since they did most of the writing down. Being a peasant didn't really change much unless the affairs of kings darkened your door.

ABOUT NAMING THE NAMES

Scottish history is populated by Scottish nobles; the Duke of Albany, the Earl of Mar, the Duke of Atholl, the Marquis of Moray etc, etc. It can get very confusing.

These are feudal lordships quite distinct in culture and practice from the Highland clans. The titles were associated with geographical areas rather than specific families, although sometimes they were maintained under the same name for generations. In the north-east, many of them hark back to ancient Pictish kingdoms. The areas of Atholl or Moray or Badenoch, or wherever, did not have fixed boundaries and grew or shrank according to local disputes. Where the line ended without an heir, the title became the gift of the king. Sometimes it was awarded to some family in the royal favour. Sometimes it was retained for one of the king's spare sons, even, on occasion, a royal bastard.

Earldom map.

When any of these noblemen had a falling out with a royal house, which was not uncommon, they lost their title and probably their head. Again the title was in the king's power and could come under new ownership or could be handed back to the next generation.

For example, the 'Earl of Mar' could be a Douglas, a Drummond, a Cochrane, an Erskine or a royal Stewart, depending on the exact date.

Sometimes titles went out of use and when reinstated they start the counting again. For instance, when the Earl of Mar turns up as a Jacobite commander in 1715 he called himself the 6th Earl but he could also be deemed the 23rd Earl.

Also, a lord could get promotion, which was not necessarily passed on. The Eighth Earl of Argyll was ALSO the 1st Marquis of Argyll. His son went back to plain Earl. The 1st Duke of Argyll was also 10th Earl.

There can be a further complication when the heir to a title holds a different title. For example, the eldest son of the Duke of Argyll is known as the Lord of Lorne (part of Argyll territory). He automatically becomes Earl (or Duke or Marquis) on his father's death. We have read histories where the same man suddenly changes name without much explanation.

There are exceptions. The Duke of Rothesay is always a Stewart. It goes to the heir apparent, just as Prince of Wales does to the English heir. In fact, the current holder is Prince Charles Windsor (he is also Earl of Carrick, Baron of Renfrew, Lord of the Isles and High Steward of Scotland). The title implied no ownership of the Isle of Bute (which did remain in the control of an endlessly colourful branch of the Stewarts).

Similarly, the Duke of Albany is always a Stewart. It was awarded to a younger son of the king. In many ways it is the most impressive title since 'Albany' is an anglicisation of 'Alba', Gaelic for Scotland. So Duke of Scotland? Despite the grandiose title, it did not come with any particular territory. Dukes of Albany were notorious for creating trouble for their fathers and brothers.

At the time of the Act of Union, when the power was in the London court, a new raft of titles were awarded, (these were often ones that had been out of use for decades) as bribes to those who supported the act. By this time these were ceremonial accolades and did not imply any land or real power.

On top of all this the families had an appalling lack of imagination when it came to Christian names. The same forename was passed from father to son again and again. If a child died in childhood his name would be recycled to a younger son.

How do you need name, rank and number?
The only way to correctly identify someone is to give the full name, rank, and number: for example, James Graham, 1st Marquis (and 5th Earl) of Montrose. This can get very clumsy. The book tries to keep things as clear as possible.

It is very helpful when there is a nickname. There may be eight Earls of Argyll (and thirteen Dukes) but there is only one 'Squinty Archie'.

ABOUT DEATH

As well as a large number of kings, there are a large number of battles. Sometimes we need to pause and think about that.

Death was more common in the Middle Ages

The quote above is attributed to a school child. While we know that the death rate is always 100 per cent, we do know what they meant; premature or violent death was more common. Those who lived through the horrors of the twentieth-century world wars or those living in any of the twenty-first-century war zones might have a different perspective (in early 2022 there are current armed conflicts in over twenty countries).

Figures that give life expectancy in Middle Age Britain as 31 years are misleading. Death in childhood was very common. This narrative is filled with unfortunate women who were forced to continue bearing heirs despite miscarriages, stillbirths and infant deaths. All involving great dangers to their own health.

If you made it to 20 you had every chance of reaching 50. Balancing the early deaths were a few who made it to 70 (William the Lion got to 72).

Infectious diseases or infection of wounds from accident or combat were the commonest causes of death. Surviving the battle might not put you in the clear; many died in the hours, days or weeks afterward.

In writing this story we are confronted with battles. While battlefield casualty numbers are very unreliable, again and again there are dozens, hundreds or thousands dead.

A king or a senior noble might have his body carried off the field for a burial with due ceremony. For the common women who had no choice but to wave their men folk off to battle there was no closure. The men simply didn't come back. They lay where they fell or were, at best, thrown into a mass grave.

Scottish folk tradition tells that if you come across a strange woman washing blood out of a shirt you will know that your love has died far away.

For many there was no word at all. The experience is captured in Karine Polwart's song:

Whaur dae ye lie, my faither?
Whaur dae ye lie, my son?
Whaur dae ye lie, my ane true love?
When will the truth be won?

THE MAKING OF SCOTLAND

ORIGINS

How is Scotland a 'Land of Fire and Ice'?

Parts of Scotland, Greenland and North America were formed in the southern hemisphere as part of the continent of Laurentia. Laurentia drifted north, crossing the equator before starting to break up. The North Atlantic Ocean began to form, leaving North America and the Scottish fragment on opposite shores. They still continue to move farther apart.

About 410 million years (about a tenth of the age of the Earth) Scotland crashed into England, explaining why the Southern Uplands are largely made up of rocks formed on the bottom of the ocean.

Over the period since, what is now Scotland has been ablaze. Many familiar landmarks are volcanoes; Ben Nevis, the Cuillin Ridge, both Arthur's Seat and Edinburgh (and Stirling) Castle Rock.

More recently, over 2½ million years, glaciers and ice sheets have invaded Scotland in at least five separate ice ages – huge forces carving the rock into landscapes we recognise today.

Truly a land of fire and ice.

How did we get here?

Scotland is a very young country: a mere 10,000 years old (to pick a round number). It had numerous eras when it had entire flora and fauna that we would not recognise. The most recent ice age 'dich't the sklate' – wiped the slate clean. The entire natural world had to restart. Every plant, invertebrate and animal had to blow in, fly in or crawl in. Including humans.

There is a common perception that a great magnificent Wild Wood grew up and then human beings arrived and spoiled it all. But it is quite possible that there were footsteps in the snow. Hunter-gatherers may have been making summer visits north during the thousands of years it took the forest to develop. Up until about 6,500 years ago they could have walked dry shod across what is now the North Sea.

Sometime after 6,000 years ago the Neolithic Era brought farming and all the disruption to the Wild Wood that that required.

The people arriving could come by boat from the Continent or by the 'Western Route' from the Mediterranean via Spain and Portugal and on up the western coast. Clear evidence that boats were involved lies in the remarkable Neolithic structures found in Orkney.

Twenty-first-century excavations have revealed a remarkable series of buildings close to the Stones of Stenness and the Ring of Brodgar. These represent a level of sophistication that was not expected. It is concluded that these structures have a religious purpose, suggesting that Orkney was a spiritual centre a thousand years before Stonehenge and long before the great Egyptian pyramids.

> BY THE WAY: The Orkney Vole has been on Orkney for over 4,500 years. It is not found anywhere else in Britain, but is found in Belgium, suggesting that it arrived as a stowaway on boats travelling directly from the Continent to the island during the Stone Age.

It was traditionally thought that Neolithic people replaced the hunter-gatherers, but now it is thought that the early folk lived alongside the farmers and then got absorbed into the new population. It was equally thought that the Bronze Age people replaced the Stone Age and then the Iron Age people replaced them. It is now thought to be more complicated than that.

INVASIONS

The first written records of north Britain were written by the Romans.

To go back before that we are in a realm where mythology and history are difficult to separate. Much of this was held in the oral tradition, handed from generation to generation by bards of some description. Such stuff is easily lost – much of it has been. Fortunately, some of this material was picked up by early medieval Christian monks, particularly in Ireland. They had their own agenda. They cobbled together bits of ancient mythology, scant existing records and a desire to tie Irish history to the period of the Old Testament and, if possible to link it to biblical landscapes and stories. Among these volumes was the *Lebor Gabala Erenn* – the Book of Invasions.

Pict.

The Book of Invasions

The Book of Invasions describes SIX different arrivals that (with varying success) attempted to dominate the island. Each group then battles with its predecessors. No dates are given, but the period roughly equates to the Old Testament era.

The penultimate group were the Tuatha de Danaan. There some ideas in their story that place them in the Bronze Age. They brought with them various 'magical' items; a magic sword, a magic spear and a magic pot. What could be more 'magic' than a metal sword, and metal-tipped spear and a metal pot if you had never seen one before.

They also brought the Lia Fail – the Stone of Destiny. The mythology links to the Bible. The stone was Jacob's pillow and the De Danaan may possibly be the Tribe of Dan, the Lost Tribe of Israel. The De Danaan then evolve into the mystical fairy folk living in a parallel universe in Ireland (and Scotland, too).

The final invasion, the successful one, was the Milesians. These have traditionally been seen as THE CELTS.

We're all Celts, aren't we?

The Celtic Invasions were well known and understood, until recently. The Celts – tall, blond, war-like, artistic people from 'East of the Danube' – headed out across Europe conquering all before them. They became the Gauls in France, the Galations in the Middle East and the Scots and Irish.

The Celts evolved along different paths, so by the time they got to Scotland there were two different groups. These could be separated by differences in the languages they left behind. These are P-Celtic, the Britons, whose linguistic legacy remains in Welsh, Cornish and Breton, and Q-Celtic, which is the root of Irish and Scottish Gaelic. The first group came across the Channel up through what is now England and occupied south and east Scotland.

The second group, the Gaelic lot (Goidelic, to use the academic term), came by the Western Route, that is by sea up the west coast of Europe, hopping from the north of Spain to the south of Ireland. There is good archaeological evidence for a strong Celtic culture in what is now Portugal and southern Spain. They would have been far enough from any original homeland to have developed a distinct language and customs.

These Celtic civilisations, divided into many warring tribes, were both well established by the time of the Romans; the Gaelic in Ireland and the west of Scotland and the Britons in the rest of the British mainland.

How does an invasion work?
Most brutally, a massive force enters a region and kills a lot of the natives and forces the survivors to flee en masse. Ethnic cleansing if you like. This is rare (you need a lot of incomers), but not unknown.

Secondly, a force enters, defeats the natives militarily and takes charge, but because most of the invaders are men they take local women as wives and form a hybrid nation. Only the men are unwanted and the invaders may have killed a good proportion of those already.

Thirdly, a force arrives and defeats the natives, then sets up new political structures that ensure the invaders are very much in control, while the locals carry on much as before (so long as they behave themselves). Two cultures exist side by side with limited interaction to begin with. This is the Roman model. Across the Roman Empire native peoples became more and more 'Romanised' but the Romans stayed Roman.

The Normans, far and away the best-documented invasion, came in with the Roman ideas and did treat their new territories as conquered lands. But they did marry local women and did merge culturally. In Ireland it was often said of the Normans who went to Ireland that they became 'more Irish than the Irish'.

The Celts were generally thought of as being Option Two. A militarily powerful elite class mingling with the locals. Or so we all thought.

How have ideas changed?
In recent times, historians have decided that this is all WRONG! We've been wrong all these years. There were NO INVASIONS! NOBODY CAME!

Rather it is argued that there was an 'Invasion of Ideas'! Technological know-how in pottery and metalworking; iron and gold, art styles and religious practices developed somewhere on the Continent invaded. These ideas then took over and dominated the culture of the native peoples. And language! People started voluntarily adopting a new vocabulary and syntax to the extent that they could no longer understand their neighbours.

Veni, Vidi, Veni – How did the Romans 'come, see and go away again'?

There is a popular misconception that the Romans came to Scotland, where they met the Picts and were so alarmed that they built a big wall to keep these painted savages out. In, fact the Romans were in Scotland for forty-three years before they started building Hadrian's Wall and built a second wall, the Antonine Wall, farther north fifty years later.

Though they could never be said to have conquered Scotland, they were around for around 300 years and there are dozens of examples of Roman presence scattered across the south of the country.

By AD 400 they had cleared out. As their forces pulled back, the 'Picts' had got bolder, striking south of Hadrian's Wall.

As the Romans retreated, Britain as a whole collapsed into what became known as the Dark Ages. It was out of this period that Alba and then Scotland would emerge. The thrust of this book is to tell that story.

BEFORE SCOTLAND

How did Scotland happen?
THE STORY THAT HAS BEEN TOLD FOR CENTURIES IS
… in the ninth century the Scots from the Kingdom of Dal Riata
went to war with the Picts under the fearsome leadership of Kenneth
MacAlpin. The Scots won – ending Pictland and wiping Pictish
culture from the face of the earth. Picts No More! The new kingdom
became Alba and then Scotland, and Kenneth MacAlpin was the first
king – the Godfather of Scotland!

This begs a few questions.

Before going any further with this it might be wise to stop and
consider who exactly was living in the northern part of Britain and
what were they up to in the few centuries preceding these events. It's
not simple! As W.C. Sellar put it in his classic *1066 and All That* …

> The Scots (originally Irish, but by now Scotch) were at this time
> inhabiting Ireland, having driven the Irish (Picts) out of Scotland;
> while the Picts (originally Scots) were now Irish (living in brackets)
> and vice versa. It is essential to keep these distinctions clearly in
> mind (and verse visa).

How did four tribes go to war?
By the end of the seventh century there were four nations in
Scotland; the Picts in the north-east, The Britons in the south-west,
the Scots of Dal Riata in the west and the Angles of Northumbria in
the south-east.

The Britons – the Kingdom of Strathclyde
We have already met the Britons, the P-Celtic speaking people. They
were occupying north Britain when the Romans arrived and they
remained here when the Romans left. It is likely that they maintained
some degree of communication with the other British strongholds

in the west of Great Britain – the lands least Romanised; Wales the West Country and the satellite colony in Brittany.

> BY THE WAY: It is somewhat ironic that, in the modern day, the folk who most likely to celebrate their 'Britishness' are the English. The Welsh, Cornish and most Scots have a far better historical claim.

The Britons occupied the whole of the south of Scotland. That changed at the start of the seventh century when the Angles invaded. If you wonder if the English ever successfully conquered and occupied Scotland, this is it! Around about 620–630 the Angles, specifically the Northumbrians, vanquished the native Britons and held power for several centuries.

But it was not all of north Britain. Not even all of southern north Britain. The British Kingdom of Strathclyde, remained.

Tribe map.

Kingdom of Strathclyde or Alt Clut

The Kingdom of Strathclyde was a fiercely independent and ferocious player in the history of north Britain for many centuries.

Strathclyde is a later name; for most of its history it was known as the Kingdom of Alt Clut. Alt Clut was the name of Dumbarton Rock, a spectacular natural fortress standing guard over the mouth of the River Clyde. The borders of the kingdom were variable, but included north and south shores of the Firth of Clyde, the Clyde Valley and some way south towards Galloway. Galloway was a separate Bretonic kingdom right up to the time of Robert the Bruce.

Most of the scant information we have about the kingdom comes from external sources. From Irish records we learn of a King Ceretic Guletic or (in latinised form) Coroticus. From a letter written by Saint Patrick himself we learn that the Alt Clutians were very early Christians, but also that they were not well behaved. Saint Patrick chastises them:

> Soldiers whom I no longer call my fellow citizens or citizens of the Roman saints, but fellow citizens of the devils, in consequence of the evil deeds; who live in death after the hostile rite of the barbarians; associates of the Scots and Apostate Picts; desirous of glutting themselves with the blood of innocent Christians, multitudes of whom I have begotten in God and confirmed in Christ.

To be effectively ex-communicated by the saint, they must already have been Christian.

Several generations on we have King Rhydderch Hael, a contemporary of Scots king Aedan Mac Gabrainn and Saint Columba. He is celebrated in Welsh chronicles for bringing an army to Wales to back Welsh lords against King Rhun Hir of Gwynedd.

These chronicles also record him at war with the Northumbrians and detail one of the many conflicts between Dal Riata and Strathclyde, 'When Aeden the Wily came to the court of Rhydderch the Generous of Alt Clut; he left neither food nor drink nor beast alive.'

Aidan is 'the Wily' and Rhyderrech is 'the Generous'. It's not hard to see whose side they were on, demonstrating that some sort of kinship between the Welsh and the north Britons existed as late as the sixth century.

When we get to AD 800 Alt Clut stands as one of the four major power blocs in north Britain.

The Anglish – the Kingdom of Northumbria

How are we not next to Sexland?

Traditional history has taught that during the sixth century there was a major invasion of Great Britain from tribes from modern-day Denmark and Germany; the Angles, the Saxons and the Jutes. But now? Maybe not!

The Anglo-Saxon invasion is another one that is under review. Opinions vary from total ethnic cleansing and population replacement to no invasion at all, just a change of fashions. One would think that this is a matter that DNA research could clear up, but unfortunately not. Two reports from the same university came up with precisely opposite conclusions.

Scotland was not directly involved in this first wave of invasion (or not invasion). The three tribes established their identity in separate territories; the Angles mostly in the east, the Saxons mostly in the south and the Jutes in Kent. They then set about warring with each other.

The territories are reflected in regional names still in use. The West Saxons were abbreviated to Wessex, East Saxons to Essex, South Saxons to Sussex. The Anglians were in East Anglia, Mercia and Northumbria.

Alfred the Great has been long regarded as the Godfather of England – he was a West Saxon. He dreamt of a United Kingdom of Anglo Saxons (which wouldn't happen till after his death). There is a story that he supported the name Angle-land in order to convince his neighbours that he was proposing a merger, not a takeover. Had he promoted his own ethnic nomenclature we would have SEXLAND as our southern neighbour instead of England.

Northumberland Wha Hae!

As far as Scotland is concerned, Northumbria is the big player. The first Anglian king recorded in the area was as early as 574. The Anglians occupied two distinct territories, Bernicia (modern Northumberland, Tyne and Wear and Durham) and Deira (modern Yorkshire). These were based on pre-existing Bretonic boundaries. The two battled it out, on and off, for decades, but out of the union came the Kingdom of Northumbria.

Expansion northward was on the agenda early with the Battle of Degastan against the Dal Riatans in AD 603. But it was King Edwin (from Deira), in power from around 616 to 633, who was most significant. While he was at constant war with his southern neighbours, the Mercians, he managed to expand Northumbrian territory north, as far as the Forth. His hold was not so secure as his successor; Oswald had to re-invade a few years after Edwin's death.

Oswald and his brother Osrui, being Bernician royalty, had fled as children when Edwin took control. They were given sanctuary by the Scots and grew up in Dal Riata. When they returned home, Osrui brought Irish/Celtic-style Christianity to the pagan Northumbrians. He imported Bishop Aidan (later Saint Aidan) from Ireland to establish the monastic settlement on Lindisfarne. Mind you, he later presided over the Synod of Whitby in 664, which rejected Celtic Christian practices and embraced the Roman Catholic

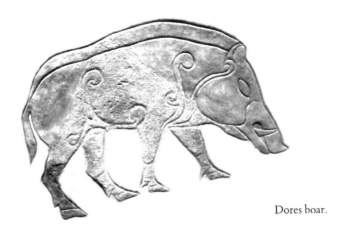

Dores boar.

From the mid-seventh century the area that is now the Scottish Borders and the Lothians was under the control of the Northumbrians. It would remain so for three centuries. They were to spend those 300 years butting heads with their neighbours the Picts, the Strathclyde Britons and the Dal Riatan Scots. Among many, many battles, the Battle of Dun Nectain in 685 against the Picts halted their expansion northwards.

In later centuries several Scottish kings would spend a lot of effort trying to absorb Northumbria into Scotland, but in AD 800 the Northumbrians held most of southern Scotland.

The Picts – the Kingdom of the Picts

The Picts have traditionally been regarded as a 'mysterious' people whose culture disappeared at the birth of Scotland. They are described as 'the Lost Tribe of Europe'.

There is an Irish story that the Picts arrived in Ireland looking for somewhere to settle. They were told that there was no room for them. They were advised that if they travelled north-east they would find a land with loads of space for them. The Picts then bypassed Ireland and made their way to what would become Scotland.

The reason for this is that they left little in the way of written records. They were far enough out of the way as to have been little noted in the vociferous Irish annals or the English chronicles.

Even their name is not helpful. 'Picts' is a hangover from the Roman 'Picti', the 'Painted People', which was a term of abuse for any northern 'barbarian'. We don't know if these people were ever happy with being referred to as Picts or when that name was assigned to them. By the fifth and sixth centuries there is absolutely no suggestion that they were kitting about covered in tattoos.

Opinion has not traditionally been kind to them, their lack of literacy generally being taken as a lack of sophistication. Attention is always drawn to their carved stonework, a primitive art form, but it was a type of expression that they took a pride in. Earlier examples show superb interpretations of animals and natural forms. When Christianity arrived, and with it literate monks with quills and ink, they did not abandon stone but rather employed it to create some magnificent examples of Christian symbols. There is an interesting interim where both Christian and Pagan traditions are celebrated on the same stones. Hedging their bets, perhaps.

How is there a 'Problem of the Picts?

In recent years archaeologists have been trying to find answers to the 'Problem of the Picts'. A huge project undertaken by the University of Aberdeen has unearthed some fascinating stories stretching over a thousand years of Pictish history.

Tap O'Noth in the Rhynie Valley near Aberdeen is now recognised as a spectacular hill fort dating back to pre-Roman times, while other settlements in the area date up to the sixth and seventh centuries. A remarkable promontory fort at Burghead was occupied right up to the tenth century. There is much more to be discovered, but it is clear that there was an ongoing culture of some sophistication for over a millennium.

For most of that time it is certain that there was no united kingdom, more likely an array of competing warlords. There is a suggestion that these coalesced into competing northern and southern regimes. By the eighth century there appears to be enough cohesion to have a Ri Picti, a King of the Picts, and enough solidarity to wage war against Scots, Northumbrians and Britons.

The most quoted reference to their language is that when Columba travelled to Inverness he had to take a translator with him. The Picts did not relate to his Gaelic. It is fair to suspect that they used a Bretonic language similar to their neighbours south of the Forth. Britons, in fact.

By 795 they were looking strong. They had been dominating the Scots for decades and keeping the Northumbrians south of the Forth.

The Scots – the Kingdom of Dal Riata

This is another story that everyone thought they knew. Around the year AD 500, Fergus Mor mac Erc and his two brothers, Loarn and Oengus, invaded from Ireland and conquered Scotland. So it was written in the poem 'Duan Albanach' – the Song of the Scots.

If there was an invasion and a horde of Irish settling in the west of

Scotland, there is no archaeological record of it. Furthermore, styles of building and even designs of brooches, supposedly brought across at this time, existed in Scotland first. It is argued that the creation of a Dal Riatan kingdom in north Britain was more a change of leadership than a military takeover.

Monarchs require justification and that requires a lineage – the more ancient the better. At the root of the line there needs to be an imposing figure, preferably a warrior king. Fergus Mor, Fergus the Great, was the man for the job, whatever his actual exploits may have been. Every King of Scots who traces his line back to Kenneth MacAlpin automatically adopts Fergus Mac Erc, Kenneth's great, great, great, great, great, great, great grandfather.

What is not denied is that the Kingdom of Dal Riata existed in the west of Scotland for the best part of 500 years and that it was culturally and politically allied with an older regime in the north of Ireland. For part of that time, but only around seventy-five years, it was under a single rule.

Around 575 the Convention of Drumceatt (held near Limavady), chaired by Columcille, established the independence of the north British kingdom from the Irish, although maintaining allegiances and responsibilities.

Where did they start from?

The story the Declaration of Arbroath tells of the Scots nation is …

It journeyed from Greater Scythia by way of the Tyrrhenian Sea and the Pillars of Hercules, and dwelt for a long course of time in Spain among the most savage peoples, but nowhere could it be subdued by any people, however barbarous. Thence it came, twelve hundred years after the people of Israel crossed the Red Sea, to its home in the west where it still lives today.

Who was Scota the Pharaoh's daughter?

The Dal Riatans were also known as 'SCOTS'. We know that the Romans used the term 'Scots' to describe those they also described as Hibernian sea pirates. The name may go back much further. The

Celtic origin story recalls Scota, an Egyptian princess: a Pharaoh's daughter. She married a Greek named Gaythius. They settled in southern Spain. Sometime later a descendant named Simon Breck brought a party of his people north. So the people of Scota, the 'Scots', arrived in Ireland. At what time this migration occurred is not known, nor is when the story was created. It does tie in with the supposed western coastal route that brought the Goidelic Q-Celtic people to Ireland.

Both these stories are closely related to the origin myths told in the Irish *Book of Invasions*.

The Dal Riatan Kingdom

Certainly, the Dal Riatans were Gaelic and it is likely that the inhabitants of western Scotland and Northern Ireland were culturally and linguistically very similar. A kingdom on two sides of the North Channel did make sense, since transport was much easier by sea than by land. On a clear day Islay is very clear to see from the Irish Dal Riatan capital, Dunseverick. The joint kingdom was by necessity a seafaring nation.

With a sea that they controlled to the west and the mountains protecting them from the east, the Scots could rest comfortably with a territory that covered modern-day Argyll and most of the Inner Hebrides.

They became a well-organised society divided into four 'Cenels'; Lorne, Kintyre, Islay and Jura, and Cowal and Bute. They were also well recorded thanks to the Irish and their own monks, who were literate in both Latin and Gaelic. They even created an early precursor to the Doomsday Book. The *Senchal fer n-Alban* was a census that recorded the status and wealth of all people in the kingdom. The object of the Norman *Doomsday Book* was to work out how much tax could be charged; the object of the *Senchal fer n-Alban* was to work out how many fighting men each community could provide. FIGHTING MEN WERE NEEDED!

Through half a millennium of history the Kingdom of Dal Riata was constantly at war! Sometimes even fighting among themselves, Cenel versus Cenel. Not only were they in conflict with the Picts, the

Northumbrians and the Strathclyde Britons, they were also obliged to turn out in support of their fellow Dal Riatans back in Ireland.

After the split from Ireland at Drumceatt, the Scots Dal Riatans were still drafted in to fight in various Irish battles, including the Battle of Fid Euin and the Battle of Magh Rath (where they fought alongside the Strathclydians) and again at the major Battle of Strathcarron (where they fought against Strathclyde). None of these went well.

Meantime, they were also facing the Northumbrians, plus centuries of ongoing enmity with the Picts, which ended up around 730 – 740 with a series of campaigns that saw Dal Riata totally defeated and occupied by their neighbours.

By the significant date of 795, the Scots were not in good shape: despite having God on their side.

How was God on their side?
One major contribution to Scottish history that the Scots are credited with was providing a foothold for Irish Christianity. Certainly they did welcome the best-known player in the game Saint Columba – Colm Cille, 'The Dove of the Church' – and gifted him a site for his mission on the Isle of Iona. Iona become a site of pilgrimage and a spiritual capital for the Celtic Church. But Columba was not the only player in the game.

Monks.

Ireland had been a crucible of fervent Christianity for over a century. It had co-opted existing traditions and developed its own unique denomination. Ireland was a land of 'Saints and Scholars'. The monasteries were places of literacy and knowledge, the monks writing in both Latin and Gaelic. It's not that they were unaware of the greater Catholic Church centred in Rome (several key figures, such as Saint Fillian, Columba's tutor, are said to have travelled to Rome), but they did retain their own set of beliefs and procedures.

Monks had different hairdos (Celtic monks shaved the front part of their heads), they calculated the date of Easter in a different way, but, fundamentally there was a difference of style. The Roman Church built up a hierarchy of priests, bishops and cardinals decked in fine robes with ornate churches and cathedrals, dripping with gold and splendour. The Celtic Church celebrated humility. A monk's life was not one of luxury, but of stony beds and constant prayer.

The Irish monks were fiercely evangelical and were audacious travellers. Around the time when Columba was born, Saint Brendan had set out on a voyage that might well have taken him to the Faroes, Iceland, Greenland and North America (500 years before the Vikings). Of course, the monks had found Scotland.

Saint Kessog from Cashel in Munster had travelled widely in Scotland, established a mission on Inchtavannach, 'Monks' Island', in Loch Lomond and been murdered (or 'martyred') on the shores of the loch before Columba was born. It was Kessog's relics that were carried into battle at Bannockburn – 'Blessed Kessog' was a battle cry for Bruce's men.

The Strathclyde Britons, with their close proximity and inevitable ties to the north-east of Ireland, had encountered and adopted Christianity at an early stage. They had their own patron saint, Saint Kentigern, also known as Saint Mungo. He founded the church that would become Glasgow Cathedral, the oldest standing building in that city. He and Columba were contemporaries. The two men are said to have met and exchanged staffs as a gesture of respect and friendship.

Nonetheless, the Dal Riata with its holy Colm Cille and his prodigies and its holy Iona was seen as a spiritual heartland of the Celtic Church.

The conversion of Northumbria was as a result of Kings Oswald and Osrui staying as guests of the Scots.

Columba did famously travel to Inverness to convert the Pictish King Bruide (the trip on which he met the Loch Ness Monster). The Scots' religious kudos may have become an important factor in the creation of Scotland.

The Stage is set

In summary, during the period from the fifth to the eighth centuries, the era traditionally known as the Dark Ages, four distinct groups existed in what is now Scotland. The boundaries were variable. The four groups were at constant war with each other. Sometimes two would pal up to hammer a third, and just as quickly fall out again. If you had a time machine and wanted to travel back to a simpler time, avoid the eighth century at all costs. It was mayhem!

At the end of that century, with a key date of 795, there is going to be a change. It's not going to get any calmer!

SCOTLAND'S START

How did Scotland's story start?
Let us jump forward a bit to round about the 840s and revisit that 'Scots conquering the Picts' and creating Scotland story. The one with Kenneth MacAlpin as the hero.

How was Kenneth 'the Conqueror'?
The story is that Kenneth became King of Dal Riata on his father's death. According to tradition, he was the great, great, great, great, great, great, great grandson of Fergus Mor who invaded from Ireland and established the kingdom. He became Ri Pictii: King of the Picts. He is popularly remembered as the first King of Scotland. Later Scottish monarchs would strain to prove they were descended from the great man. So were all the Kings of England! For every English monarch tracing their ancestry back to Henry I (William the Conqueror's son), also traces it to Malcolm Canmore. Henry was married to Matilda, Malcolm's daughter. Malcolm was, of course, the great, great, great, great, great grandson of Kenneth MacAlpin.

It was important to show him as a magnificent, noble and fearsome. Years after his death, he was given the title Cinead an Ferbasach, Kenneth the Conqueror. The image of him in the 'Famous Scots' Frieze in the Scottish National Portrait Gallery shows him as the perfect image of a tall, handsome warrior.

> BY THE WAY: Since Kenneth was directly descended from Fergus Mor, all the following kings were originally Irish!

How does he measure up? If he was a 'Conqueror' where are the great military campaigns, the great battles? One story told of his ascent to power in Pictland is none too noble. It was said that he invited the Pictish nobility to a party at Scone, and the magic number of 'seven' Pictish lords turned up. He got them sloshed and while they were in the midst of drunken revelry he sprung his trap. His men pulled pins from the benches on which the Picts were sitting. The benches collapsed and they were flung back into prepared pits lined with sharpened blades. It was an easy job to finish them off. A great movie scene – a 'Red Wedding'!

There was a very important battle in this sequence of events but Kenneth MacAlpin wasn't even there! At this major battle in Fortrui the Picts lost heavily. The king and most of the chief figures in the hierarchy were slain, leaving the leadership up for grabs.

> BY THE WAY: Fortrui was a region that would become, roughly, the Earldom of Moray and modern Morayshire. It was a Pictish heartland.

Kenneth MacAlpin.

At this point it's as well to remember that Kenneth's mum was a Pictish princess, as the story goes. Remember too that kingship did not go by eldest son; candidates could be selected from anyone of royal blood and, thanks to his mother, Kenneth was. He was a contender, an outside bet in the first place, but a contender and he had support. Recent thinking suggests that Scots from Dal Riata had been drifting eastwards away from their homeland for decades, moving under pressure from an outside source. They were essentially refugees seeking shelter. By the time Kenneth was vying for leadership the Scots were already becoming a significant force within Pictland.

God on his side
Kenneth had God, or at least the church, on his side. Colum Cille, Saint Columba, had the credit for the early evangelising of the Picts. Pictish stone works document the arrival of Christianity with monuments featuring both Pagan and Christian stories. Development of the faith had stayed in the west, creating the unique Celtic Christianity centred on Iona. Picts and Scots shared the faith but the Scots had the enhanced version, although Iona, in particular, was under grave threat.

Plus, if at any time it made sense for two nations to pool resources, it made sense in the 830s and '40s. It was at this time, in 834, that a joint Pict and Scots force met a Northumbrian army under an Aethelstan. Eochaid, Scots king, spotted a strange cloud formation, a diagonal cross against a blue sky. It reminded him of St Andrew's cross. He prayed to the saint and the battle was won.

There is not much evidence of Kenneth Canmore being a conquering hero, nor is there much sense of the Picts being a defeated race. There is a coming together of the refugee Scots and the Picts to form a new united entity. This Scot–Pict Alliance evolved into the Kingdom of Alba, which would become the Kingdom of Scotland.

The Scots did have a major cultural impact with the Gaelic language overtaking the Bretonic and Iona-based Gaelic Christianity becoming dominant.

BY THE WAY: The usual evidence given for the existence of both languages is in place names. The most quoted example is the word for 'RIVER', which is 'ABER' in Bretonic, as in ABERdeen and in Wales ABERystwyth as opposed to 'INVER' as in INVERness and in Dal Riatan INVERary.

How did Scotland forget its own past?

Just how powerful this 'cultural takeover' of the Scots was is revealed in Scotland's great statement of nationhood – the Declaration of Arbroath in 1320. It tells the ancient origin story of the migration from Scythia, which is the Irish/Dal Riatan version, and it states of the Scottish nation, 'The Britons it first drove out, the Picts it utterly destroyed.'

It totally denies the heritage of the majority of people in north Britain and the nations that had merged just 300 years earlier.

However this coming together played out at the time, Kenneth is the figurehead who gets the credit. The nation needed a fearsome founding father figure. If Kenneth MacAlpin didn't exist he would have had to be invented. Which is pretty much what happened!

Why did things change at this time?

Scots were abandoning their homeland and drifting east into Pictish territory, BECAUSE OF THE VIKINGS!

The symbols and treasures of Celtic Christianity needed a new home, BECAUSE OF THE VIKINGS!

The Pictish lords had been killed in battle, BY THE VIKINGS!

The Scots and Picts joining forces made sense, BECAUSE OF THE VIKINGS!

If anyone 'MADE SCOTLAND HAPPEN' it was the VIKINGS!

795 AND ALL THAT

This book chooses AD 795 as a starting point for the evolution of the disparate tribes of north Britain into the nation of Scotland. It is a hugely significant date in Scottish history; it was the first appearance of the Norse in Scotland. They raided the Abbey of Iona (Lindisfarne had been the very first attack two years earlier).

> BY THE WAY: The term 'Viking' is completely misused. Its root is a verb 'to go Viking', meaning to head out to raid. Any Scandinavian peaceably going about his business should not be addressed as 'Viking'. The Annals refer to the raiders as 'Genti' or the 'Gentiles', co-opting a biblical term to mean 'Heathen or Pagan'.
>
> The name 'Norse' is better, though it is itself a generalisation for Norwegian, Swedish and Danish folk.

The 'VIKING ERA' is the first time in Scottish history that we can actually put firm dates to an age. It started with the Iona raid in 795 and ended with the Treaty of Perth on 2 July 1266. 471 years!

This was no hit and run affair.

The Treaty of Perth saw King Harold IV of Norway officially relinquish the Scottish mainland, the Hebrides and the Isle of Man to Alexander III of Scotland. Vikings No More! But it's not that simple.

The early raids were just that – smash (murder) and grab! Then they'd go home and come back again next summer, or the summer after. These attacks must have been utterly terrifying; heavily armed warriors slaughtering unarmed monks – 'Wolves among sheep', as an English chronicle put it.

How was the Scot's Land lost?

Northumbria's Holy Island of Lindisfarne took the first strike but it was Dal Riata that was most vulnerable. For men from the fjords of Norway, the west coast sea lochs and islands must have seemed very comfortable terrain. They hit Iona in 795 and Rathlin Island in Irish Dal Riata in the same year, and Iona again in 802 and 806 and 825. Soon they weren't just making flying visits – the first record of a Norse army staying for the winter was in 839.

It is likely that the Scots moving east across north Britain were fleeing as refugees from the Vikings rather than invading the Picts. With their spiritual capital of Iona under such repeated attack, the treasures, relics, artefacts and, most importantly, documents, had to be spirited away. Some went to Ireland, including the fabulous *Book of Kells* (not necessarily a smart move, Ireland was also under massive attack). Others went across to form new religious centres at Scone and Dunkeld, including the 'Stone of Destiny'. These may have seemed a bit safer from attack by sea, at least at first.

The Scots were not the only ones under attack. In a huge battle in Fortrui (around Moray) the Picts lost heavily, against the Norse. Many of the leading Pictish chieftains were killed. This may have been a key event in allowing Kenneth MacAlpin to come to prominence – the competition had been felled by Viking axes.

Much has been made of the disappearance of Pictland. But if you look at it, it was actually Dal Riata – 'the Scot's Land' that was lost – abandoned to the Vikings. In east northern Britain the Alban Alliance saw Pictish culture being somewhat hijacked by the Scots. The Picts didn't go anywhere.

We'll come back to what happened in the west.

Longship.

How did the Vikings not go home?

Once the Norse had firmly decided that buckets loads of silver and trinkets were all very well but what a growing population in the relatively poor agricultural landscape of Scandinavia needed was LAND to settle on, it was a different game.

The Scottish nations did not fair all that badly.

The English suffered much worse – a huge proportion of the country was lost to the Norse. By the 880s Danelaw stretched from the Tees to the Thames. Their ownership of this vast land-holding, close enough to half of the Anglo-Saxon territories, was recognised in a treaty with Alfred, Godfather of England.

Ireland did not fare much better. The Norse settled on a Black Pool (a Dubh Linn) on the east coast and extended their territories from there. The Norwegian Kings of Dublin would be major players for hundreds of years.

> BY THE WAY: The north coast of Ireland (after some early raids) largely avoided invasion. There is some evidence that they developed some sort of 'rapid response force' that kept the Vikings at bay. The authors wonder if this might be related to the legends of Finn MacCool and the Fianna. It is not known when the cycle of Finn stories was created but it is likely to have been some time after this period. Memories of a real-life hero and his guerrilla war band might have contributed.

Parts of the territories did come under Scandinavian control: the Northern Isles, Shetland and Orkney would not be recognised by anyone as 'Scottish' for centuries yet.

The north coast was lost. Some of the most northerly land in Great Britain is still called 'SUTHerland' because to the Scots it may be north, but to the Scandinavians it was definitely 'South-Land'.

The west was lost. All of the former Dal Riata, the rest of the Mainland coast, the Inner and Outer Hebrides were de facto Scandinavian for a couple of centuries. Scotland (part of it) was invaded, conquered and settled by a foreign force – the Norwegians.

While England, by and large, got Danes – Scotland (and Ireland) got Norwegians. The Swedes went east and left their name, the 'Russe', on a significant part of northern Asia!

Strathclyde, with its extensive seaboard on the Clyde, was an obvious target. Alt Clut itself (Dumbarton Rock), was a major obstacle. The natural feature is impressive and generation after generation had added constantly evolving defences. The usual word to describe the like is 'impregnable'. There was no way the Vikings were going to storm it. What the Dublin Vikings did in 870 was to take a leaf out of someone else's playbook. They laid siege. It was very un-Viking behaviour; they were used to charging in with 'shock and awe', putting the fear of Thor into their opponents and overwhelming with axe and sword. It wasn't going to work here! They changed tactics and starved the Britons out (who hadn't planned for this).

The defeat was a huge blow to the Kingdom of Alt Clut. Forced off their beloved rock, they assembled a new capital in Govan (home of Glasgow's shipyards) and had to accept being 'Strathclyde' instead of 'Alt Clut'. It was a huge blow.

However ...
The Northumbrians managed to survive as a sovereign region. They lost the south of their kingdom (formerly Deira), which hosted the major Norse city of Jorvik (York), but kept their hold on north-east England and south-east Scotland.

The Albans (the Scots–Pict Alliance) largely held the east, north of Forth.

ALBA

Following Kenneth MacAlpin there were seven kings of Picts in less than fifty years. Some of them didn't last very long. Donald I, Kenneth's brother, lasted for four years.

Constantin I, Kenneth's son, managed fifteen years. He was in power when the huge 'Great Heathen Army' was devastating England. When two Ireland-based Norse brothers decided to push into Fortrui, Constantin I may have tried to pay them off. There was some disagreement over a proposed marriage, possibly with Constantin's sister, in which the two Viking brothers fell out and Amlaib killed his own sibling (this was the same guy who besieged Alt Clut the following year).

When Amlaib returned for a further payout, Constantin got the better of it and Amlaib lost his head. By 875 the Vikings were back. Constantin was captured and beheaded, possibly on the beach at Fife Ness.

King Aed was also a son of Kenneth. We don't know much about him except that he is referred to in different sources as the gentle and poetic 'Aed of the White Flowers' and as 'Aed the Furious'. He didn't last a year. The Annals of Ulster report that he was killed by his 'associates'.

Then we have a Giric and an a Eochaid, who ruled jointly. Then a Donald II, killed by Vikings at Dunnottar. Then in 900 we have Constantin II, grandson of Kenneth. The ACTUAL First King of Alba!

How did we actually get a King of Alba?

Constantin II, Kenneth's grandson, is the bloke who finally gets the title 'King of Alba': he is the first king from northern Britain who moves on an international stage. He also achieved the very rare feat for a Scottish king (in any period) of dying of old age.

Vikings were top of the agenda from the start of Constantin's rule. The young man's first challenge was when a Norse force punched through as far as Dunkeld, but were defeated in Strathearn. Later he joined the Northumbrians in a major but inconclusive battle on the banks of the Tyne.

But Constantin would be the first to face a new challenge and he wouldn't be the last – ENGLAND.

Alfred the Great died with his son Edward as King of Wessex and his daughter Aethelflaed as the 'Lady of Mercia'. They pursued his dream of a united Angleland. They were followed by Aethestan (not the Saltire one – same name, different guy). Aethelstan had his own agenda. He fixed a truce with Daneland that gave him the freedom to attack Northumbria instead. He took over much of their territory, including land north of the Tweed.

Not satisfied, he moved further north, defeating King Owain of Strathclyde and pushing into Alban country. What accommodation was made is not clear but when Aethelstan went home, Constantin travelled with him. It was one of several trips he made to the English court, where he was honoured as an important person. Some English documents refer to him as a 'Sub-King', but there is evidence that he officially kow-towed to Aethelstan.

Constantin II.

The Great Battle

Matters were clearly not resolved and came to a brutal head. In 937 Constantin allied with Owain of Strathclyde. They were both under threat from England. More surprising was that joining the Alliance were the Dublin Norse: Scots and Britons were fighting alongside their long-time Viking enemies. They marched south with a huge force. Aethelstan met them with an equally impressive army in the Battle of Brunnanburh. It was known for years after as 'The Great Battle'. The Annals of Ulster describes, 'a great battle, lamentable and terrible was fought … in which fell uncounted thousands of the Northmen … and on the other side a multitude of Saxons fell.'

Just how many thousands were 'uncounted' we don't know but it was a huge and very bloody affair. Aethelstan claimed the victory, but enough damage seems to have been done to the military resources of all sides that there was an (uneasy) peace for a time.

Aethelstan died and the new England fell to pieces under renewed attacks from the Irish Norse.

Constantin had had enough. He abdicated in favour of his nephew, Malcolm I, and retired to a monastery at St Andrews to live out his days in peace. He had ruled for forty-three years – a record at the time. He was the first King of Alba and it was during his reign that the terms Scot and Scotland were first written.

Fifty years on

In the following half century there were no fewer than eight kings of Alba. Mostly short and bloody reigns. By the time we get to 1005 and the start of the eleventh century we have Malcolm II on the stone. The kingdom of Strathclyde was still strong. The Northumbrians were still in the south-east. The Vikings were still a threat (he had to face of an invasion by the English Norse King Cnut).

Malcolm did manage twenty-nine years as king. The title passed to Duncan I, who is most famous for his death in Act II.

How was there a dagger before him?

Our theme has been that how you get remembered depends on how your story is told and on WHO tells your story, but sometimes it is very important to consider WHO THEY ARE TELLING IT TO!

There is a medieval King of Scots who is extremely well known, but whose name never comes up in answer to 'What Scottish kings have you heard of?' Perhaps because people are not sure if he was real. Macbeth was Ri an Alba, King of Alba from 1040 to 1057. He was very real!

The reason that he is known to most people is due to a telling of his story 600 years after his death. William Shakespeare took some pretty sketchy Scottish history and wrote a play, 'the Scottish Play', with the very deliberate intention of pleasing his new ultimate boss – a King of Scots (and now England).

Let's look at the plot.

A 'rightfu' king' of Scots is murdered by scurrilous and deceitful means. King James I had escaped death by sneaky methods in the 'Gunpowder plot' just a few years before.

The whole enterprise was inspired by WITCHES. James was paranoid about attack from witches and was very vigorous in curtailing them (mostly by burning alive).

Mac Beth.

The evil action was driven by an unhinged woman. James was never comfortable with females.

The witches' demonic prophesies are overturned. The rampant lady gets her comeuppance. The aspiring usurper is slain.

Result? One happy monarch and patronage in the pocket of the playwright.

The real story of Mac Bethad mac Findlaích is somewhat different.

Shakespeare's MacBeth has been played by many, many actors in many, many different costumes. Few, if any, reflect the description given of him in 'The Prophecy of Berchán', 'The red, tall, golden-haired one, he will be pleasant to me among them'. He was a ginger!

Disputed kingdom

When he appears in the story he is Mormaer of Moray (forerunner of the Earls of Moray), which puts him fair and square in what used to be Pictland. Norman influence is yet to come, so Celtic traditions still apply. The king can be selected from the pool of sons who have royal blood. There was a tradition that the choice was alternated between two branches of the family. Malcolm II tried to ignore the agreement, and installed his own son, Duncan, instead of MacBeth, whose turn it was. So Macbeth had every right to be miffed!

Then Duncan got miffed with MacBeth. Duncan had led an attack into England, which was a disaster and he needed somebody to blame. Duncan led a military assault on Moray. Mayhem ensued in which Duncan ended up 'deid'. He died on the battlefield aged around 40. NOT an old man murdered in the dead of night.

MacBeth became king without much opposition, since he was a legitimate candidate for the post, and ruled for seventeen years over a prosperous and, largely, peaceful Scotland. He may have travelled all the way to Rome to meet the Pope. To be away from your kingdom for the time it took to make that journey meant you were feeling secure.

But, of course, things come back to bite you! The deid Duncan's queen and his son had fled, probably to her family in Northumbria. Resentment simmered and bubbled. When the time was right Duncan's son, Malcolm, enlisted a large force of Northumbrians to march north. In a battle at Dulsinnan (Shakespeare's Dulsinane) they surprised MacBeth's position by creeping around in the woods. It was a substantial bloodbath with accounts suggesting there were over 4,000 deaths. Malcolm won!

In a follow-up skirmish at Lumphannon, MacBeth fell. The story goes that the deeply injured MacBeth was carried to Scone, where he died in the coronation place, the centre of Scotland. It's a good story. He was succeeded by his stepson. If you want a quiz answer to the most obscure Kings of Scots, then this boy, King Lulach, would be a good answer. He only lasted a few months before Malcolm caught up with him, slaughtered him and took the crown.

SCOTLAND AT LAST

MacBeth has been described as the last CELTIC king, the last Ri an Alban. In 1058 Malcolm III was crowned as Ri an Alban but, during his reign he changed the language of the court from Gaelic to Scots. His title became King of Scots. His name at least is one of the best remembered of early monarchs. He became Malcolm Canmore!

Great Chief, King of Scots
Ceann Mor literally translates as 'Big Head', but in this context is usually rendered as 'Great Chief'. His name is remembered, but not so much what made him great. There is not that much really. He led several campaigns south of the border, never with much ambition to tackle England as a whole. He seemed more intent in adding Northumbria to Scotland. He failed and died in battle at Alnwick.

What was most remarkable about him was his family: his first marriage was to a Viking lady of royal blood. His second would become not just a notable queen, she became a saint. Margaret was of the Royal House of Wessex. Fleeing the Normans, she sought shelter in Scotland and married the king. Her religious fervour had a huge influence on the Scottish church – St Margaret's Chapel was built in her honour, probably by her son, David. It is the oldest standing part of Edinburgh Castle.

Malcolm III was the father of no fewer than four kings and a queen of England (whose daughter would become not a queen, but an empress).

Before we get to any of these we have to keep an eye on the dates. Malcolm became king in 1058 and eight years later he was already married to Ingibiorg Finnsdottir and had a son and heir. That year was 1066. It was an important date.

1066 and all that

Very briefly; the Norse were not only a big issue in the British Isles, they were big news in France. The King of France may have been known as Charles the Simple, but he wasn't daft. Rather than stand

Canmore and Margaret.

yet another attack, he gave a substantial chunk of his north-west to the Vikings on the condition that they defended him, principally from other Vikings, and that they converted to Christianity. These people, now the Normans (North Men), embraced the new religion enthusiastically.

Several generations on, during a dynastic lapse, one young man established himself as a leader and military commander. He was known as William the Bastard. The name indicates a familial situation that was a major stumbling block to many would-be rulers – but not to William.

In 1066 he brought boatloads of heavily armed knights across La Manche and won the (very) bloody Battle of Hastings, was crowned King of England – and that was that! Except it wasn't. There were years of bloody battles and brutal oppression to quell England; and then there was Wales; and there was Ireland. He did a lot of damage, but he could now, fairly, be called William the Conqueror. As for Scotland? We'll come to that.

Malcolm's dynasty

Malcolm III is one of the best-remembered medieval kings; not for any great achievements but for the dynasty that followed him. Just as he was descended from Kenneth MacAlpin, every subsequent Scottish monarch is descended from Malcolm Canmore – and nearly every English one.

He was father to four kings of Alba; Edgar, Edmund, Alexander I and David I. AND A QUEEN OF ENGLAND. His daughter, Matilda of Scotland, married England's Henry I. Every succeeding English king, apart from the usurper Henry VII, has Malcolm as a forebear. (Henry VII took care to marry Elizabeth of York, a genuine Royal, so Henry VIII and family were back in the family tree thanks to their mum).

Also remember that since Malcolm's wife, Margaret of Wessex, was of the English royal line all the Scottish kings are also heirs to the English throne.

These lineages may seem dull but at times they become very important indeed.

THE KING WHO
SAVED SCOTLAND

With the death of Malcolm III (Canmore) fighting Northumbrians at the Battle of Alnwick in 1093, we are now in the Middle Middle Ages and a period when we can actually start talking about Scotland.

After Malcolm's brother Donald III had a brief shot, it was now up to his brood of (first) millennial offspring to kick the ball around. Duncan II was first up. He had taken the unexpected step of joining the Normans, qualified as a bona fide Norman knight and fought alongside William the Conqueror. His only son went under the Norman name of William FitzDuncan. He became a Mormaer of Moray.

King Edgar (another son of Malcolm) lasted only a few years and was followed by Alexander I. Alexander had one son, Malcolm MacAlexander, who was illegitimate but nonetheless had a role to play in the following decades. Despite strenuous efforts, he never got to be king.

But it was Malcolm's youngest son, David, who you should remember. If you count importance of a regime on how much they actually CHANGED the country, then David I has got to be very close to the top: David was the man who saved Scotland.

While his father had established Scotland as a COUNTRY in the eyes of his neighbours, David established it in the eyes of Europe.

How did David save Scotland?
You might think that William the Conqueror fought the Battle of Hastings, King Harold got an arrow in the eye (or not) and it was all over bar the shouting! The 'shouting' lasted decades and was bloody and brutal.

Everywhere in England opposition was ruthlessly stamped out. A network of motte and bailey castles were quickly erected to emphasise and enforce the occupation. The north of England was particularly stubborn and so was particularly savagely dealt with – it was destroyed. In a winter campaign in 1069, seventy men, women, children and animals were murdered. Stores, crops and whole villages were burnt. The whole region was devastated. Sixteen years later when the *Domesday Book* would try to assess the value of every section of the country, large swathes of the north were still producing nothing. Figures in the region of 100,000 dead are suggested.

It was called the 'Harrying of the North'. David saved Scotland from that.

One effect on Scotland was that the Kingdom of Northumbria, which had ruled south-east Scotland for centuries, was cut off at the root.

The Norman campaigns in Wales were savage and would drag on for generations. David saved Scotland from that.

The Irish king Dairmid MacMurragh invited Normans to help in a local dispute – they liked the place so much they stayed. In a short time a succession of Norman lords seized their own chunks of land, overpowering and replacing many of the native lords. David saved Scotland from that.

How?

During the squabbles between his brothers and his Uncle Donald, David had headed to England. His wee sister, Matilda, had married Henry, William the Conqueror's son, so he had an in at court. He got a proper Norman education and trained as a Norman knight, firstly under King William Rufus.

After David's brother, Edgar, had come to an accord with England, David was bequeathed some land, quite a chunk! He was given what is now the Scottish Borders, much of the Lothians and Lanarkshire – basically the lands that had formerly been controlled by the now defunct Kingdom of Northumbria. Cumbria was part of the package; in fact his title was Prince of the Cumbrians.

When David's other brother, Alexander, died, David pressed his claim to the Scottish kingship. He had the backing of his brother-in-law, now King Henry I of England.

David's nephew, Malcolm, bastard son of Alexander, objected and there followed ten years of civil war. Malcolm kept losing to David's forces (which were heavily supported by England), but somehow kept escaping capture. Finally he was caught and taken to Roxburgh castle, never to be seen again. David could finally claim to be King of Scots in actuality, not just in name. In fact, with his hold on former Pictland, former Northumbrian territory and much of what had been the Kingdom of Strathclyde, he was king of a far bigger swathe of north Britain than any man before him.

David I.

How were events in England important?

Events in England now took a turn for the violent. On Henry I's death his only surviving child was a girl, Matilda. The plan was that she would succeed, however her cousin, Stephen, had other ideas and declared himself king. David I declared for his niece Matilda (but kept his own interests in mind). Three times he invaded England; twice he settled with some advantageous land settlements and avoided battle; the third time he meant business. English chroniclers made a lot of the savagery of this campaign, even describing it as a 'harrying'.

After a small victory at Clitheroe, he met Stephen's army in the Battle of the Standard near the River Tyne. David had a far superior force but he lost – he was not out of the game, however, but sat at the negotiating table again. Stephen kept the castles at Bamburgh and Newcastle, but David kept Carlisle and his son, another Henry, got the Earldom of Northumbria. David was happy enough.

When Matilda returned from exile for another bash at Stephen, David was nominally on her side, but effectively he used the chaos to regain Newcastle and Bamburgh and consolidate his hold on the north of England.

How did King David give Scotland away?

If an 'invasion' can be defined as a cultural takeover rather than a military occupation, then here was the Norman invasion of Scotland! All at the command of its own king. The entire structure of land ownership, government and the church was completely upended.

The ownership of the very fabric of the country: the land, was under new a new regime – FEUDAL LAW! Land was no longer something that was the birthright of families with generations of blood and sweat invested, it was now a commodity: it could be acquired or lost; it could be bought or sold. The owner need no longer have ancient ties to the land nor any responsibility for his tenants – he need only have the clout to hold on to it.

Royal Burghs, on Norman lines, were created. Starting with Berwick and Roxburgh, David granted fifteen of them. These were to be trading centres with a strict set of rules. They did promote economic growth, but they also created a structure for collection of a new construct – TAX!

Every man had always had responsibilities to his chieftain and his neighbours (mostly in providing fighting men), but this tax was a national institution. In order to make the new system work 'Sheriffdoms' appeared with royally empowered officials to enforce the rules. This was no longer some local hard man getting his way: these sheriffs had the might of the state behind them.

Motte and bailey castles sprang up to emphasise and implement the power of the state. The building of (Norman style) castles began. Sure, there had always been defensive structures; raths, duns and brochs, but this was on a different scale.

Religion was transformed, too. David was praised and made a saint for his promotion of the church. Monasteries sprang up. These had often very substantial land holdings and, in due course, magnificent buildings. They were gifted to imported orders (Cistercians and Augustinians) with foreign practices and procedures. It was very much part of the Church of Rome.

It was a far cry from the humble ascetics of the Gaelic–Celtic Christianity of Columba.

And it was not just the Gaelic church and Gaelic structures that were left behind – the language went too. The king and his nobles would have conversed in Norman French, while the language of the marketplace, the new Burghs, became English.

David did not accomplish all this in his lifetime, but he set it in motion. It is known as the 'Normanisation of Scotland' or the 'Davidian Revolution'. David the First, King of Scotland, gave his entire country over to a foreign culture!

Since these changes reflected what was happening on the Continent, Scotland could now be seen as a civilised country. It was no longer a barbarous horde on the fringes steeped in its own ancient and mysterious customs: it could be a European country.

How did the Normans get here?
David didn't just import ideas. He imported people, too!

David imported monks and tradesmen to bolster trade, such as the lucrative Borders wool trade, but more significantly he imported noblemen! He did owe a debt to the Normans who had supported him and make his actual control of Scotland possible; some needed to be rewarded.

But a driving reason was that he needed to replace the Scots–Pictish and Bretonic chieftains who, not surprisingly, were objecting to his onslaught against the existing culture. He needed to move fast, while he had the upper hand militarily.

Out of this came the major power families of Scotland who would dominate Scotland for the next 700 years!

Some arrived directly from Normandy, Flanders or Brittany.

Some had blatantly 'foreign' names like de Comyn, de Bailleul, de Brus or FitzAlan. These names usually became slightly moderated.

Some had had some alteration beforehand. An example is the Norman Earls of Mellent, who had fought at the Battle of Hastings and were already established in England as lords, brought the placename of their English lands north as de Hambledon. Hamilton!

Some took up a regional name. Murray obviously relates to the Scottish place of Moray (formerly the Pictish heartland of Fortrui). The family's founder, Freskin, is sometimes claimed to have been from ancient Pictish stock, but given his arrival (around King David's time) it is very likely he was Norman or Flemish.

How do you judge David I?

The First Norman Invasion of Scotland was overwhelming! Culture, governance and religion had been overturned. Power at national and local level was in the hands of foreigners; the descendants of these Normans would dominate Scotland from then on.

The Normans would be back, but then that would be Scotto-Normans against Anglo-Normans – with the Scotto-Normans praying that the people would support them!

As to David I? The man who saved Scotland from the savagery of the full-on Norman war machine. The man who put Normans in all the key positions in the kingdom. The man who dragged Scotland out of the Dark Ages and made it a European country. The man who tried to wipe out the existing Scots–Pictish–Bretonic culture, and would have called it 'Progress'.

Judge him as you will.

But if you want to judge kings by how much they changed the country then David I is hugely important.

THE LION

David's son, Henry Earl of Northumbria, was already dead when his father died. A grandson, Malcolm IV, known as the 'Virgo' (which was not a reference to his star sign) stepped in for a few years. He was dead by the age of 24: with obviously no children. He was followed by his brother William I – 'THE LION'.

How did Scotland get given away, again?

William the Lion's long-term conviction was that Northumbria should be part of Scotland and he tried in various ways to make it so. It all came to grief when he supported a rebellion against Henry II led by Henry's own wife and son, Richard the Lionheart. William's asking price for a military intervention was, of course, Northumbria; his father's territory.

William.

He marched south, but only got as far as Alnwick. He was with only a small band of men when he was ambushed, but nonetheless charged headlong into Henry II's troops. Needless to say he had no chance – he was captured and dragged in chains all the way to Valaise in Normandy.

In order to be released, William signed a document, The Treaty of Valaise. Among the provisions were ...

> William, king of Scots, has become liegeman of the lord king (Henry) against every man in respect of Scotland and in respect of all his other lands ...
> And all the bishops and abbots and clergy of the king of Scots and their successors shall do fealty to the lord king (Henry) as to their liege lord ...
> The earls also and barons and such other men holding land from the king of Scots as the lord king Henry may select, shall also do homage to the lord king ...

He had signed himself up as a subordinate to the King of England. He had signed over the entire structure of the Christian Church in Scotland. He had committed every nobleman, indeed every land owner, in Scotland to be subservient to the King of England.

Furthermore, he signed over the castles of Edinburgh, Stirling, Roxburgh, Jedburgh and Berwick – and he sent twenty prominent nobles, including his own brother, to England as hostages.

This might sound to you like a total capitulation: that's what it is. King William I had signed over Scotland to the English. Scotland was now a vassal state!

So how did he get out of that one?

The answer is that fifteen years later he bought it back. Richard the Lionheart was now on the English throne. Remember that William had been captured, at least nominally, supporting Richard against his own father. Richard, despite being well known as an English king, perhaps because of his traditional cameo appearances in all the Robin Hood movies, spent very little time in England. He preferred to spend his time securing his territories in France. Or, even better, heading off on jaunts to slaughter Muslims in the Middle East.

Killing infidels and the 2,000-mile trip to do it costs a lot of money. Richard needed a lot of ready cash. Scotland was pretty low on his agenda so he sold it back to William for 10,000 merks sterling.

The Treaty of Valaise, William's humiliation, was annulled, cancelled, gone. But it was not forgotten.

William was older than Richard the Lionheart, but also outlived him by many years. He had the distinction of being the longest-serving King of Scots, a remarkable forty-nine years (1165–1214), up until Jamie Saxt (the sixth). William had his own impact on the history of the Scots, but failed in his lifetime ambition to have a major impact on the history of Northumbria.

David I had surrendered Scotland to a foreign culture, but it can be argued that he did so in the genuine belief that it was desirable (or at least inevitable). However, it pretty much looks like William the Lion signed away Scotland to save his own skin. Not much of a roar!

How did the border get where it is?
Alexander II, William's son, was involved in various conflicts with the Norse and the Gal Gael. His most notable contribution to Scottish history was the 'Treaty of York' with King Henry III. It gave away the claim to Northumbria, which had been held by his grandfather, and Cumbria and Westmorland that his great grandfather David had once ruled.

The treaty pretty much drew the border where it is now (apart from Berwick-upon-Tweed, which would change hands a few times).

Alexander III followed. He was the man who finally 'beat' the Vikings. But we have a few things to consider before we get to that.

END OF THE VIKINGS

Alexander III is famous for two things – falling off his horse and defeating the Vikings (but not in that order).

The Vikings had not gone away. While the Gal Gael were fighting their own corner, the full-on Norwegian Vikings still held the Isle of Man and much of the Hebrides. Alexander III wanted to add all this to Scotland. The popular story is that he defeated a massive Viking force at the Battle of Largs and won the disputed lands; it was, of course, not as simple as that.

In the first place he asked nicely. In negotiations he asked, demanded and offered bribes to the Norwegian King Haakon IV. Haakon was not amenable to this style of politics. We don't know how much of an offensive he expected from the Scottish king but he decided to get his retaliation in first. His response was to assemble a massive armada and sail into the Firth of Clyde. Ships and troops were brought all the way from Norway; he had foot soldiers and even cavalry, but they were all on the boats.

At first a small local force faced them on the shore, soon joined by Alexander and his main army. Alexander launched into his favoured tactic – talking. He kept up a barrage of claims and offers, prolonging the negotiations while waiting for his greatest ally to arrive – the weather!

Viking battle.

It was 30 September when the storm hit. Several Norse ships were driven on to the beach; Scottish archers picking off the struggling crews. Haakon's hand was forced and he hurriedly sent soldiers ashore without any great evidence of a strategy. One body had made it to some higher ground, but realised that they were about to be cut off from their brothers still on the beach: they fell back to keep a united force. The guys on the beach saw them retreating and thought it was a general rout. They turned and headed back to their ships – now it was a general rout! Haakon gathered his ships and pulled back to the Hebrides. Injured but not badly hurt; he would be back (or so he thought).

Having been thwarted by the weather once, a seaborne attack in winter seemed foolish; it could wait till spring. Rather than heading home, he settled on the safe haven of Orkney.

The Battle of Largs had turned back Haakon's campaign of 1263, but had by no means devastated the Vikings. What happened in Orkney was probably more significant. The bold King Haakon IV took ill and died.

How did the Vikings go home?

Haakon's son, Magnus Haakonarson, took his place. Norway was a very different place from the wild land from which independent Jarls had launched the first attacks on Britain. It was now a sovereign country, though it was plagued by as many civil wars for control as anywhere else.

Magnus was a very different man to his father. He was a deeply Christian moderniser, dedicated to 'improving' Norway: he was a peacemaker. He made a peace accord with Henry III of England and even came to agreement with neighbouring Sweden and confirmed a permanent border.

He was just the man for Alexander to talk to!

Three years after Haakon's death they talked. What cards had Alexander to deal with? What could he offer? Not a lot, but money talks.

With the Treaty of Perth, Alexander bought the Hebrides and the Isle of Man from Magnus (Norway retained Shetland and Orkney).

A lump sum of 4,000 Merks, plus an annual charge of 100 Merks. Whether he got a bargain or not would remain to be seen.

The year was 1266 and the 'Viking Era' was ended: the Norse had gone home!

But, of course, they hadn't. Viking DNA, Viking culture and Viking spirit was woven deeply, blood and bone, into the people of west and north Scotland. That would have an impact for centuries to come.

How did a horse change Scottish history?

Alexander would later arrange the marriage of his daughter, Margaret, to Magnus's son, Eric II of Norway. He had another son who died young, but he still had a healthy heir, another Alexander. When this boy died, Alexander had to act quickly: he was only aged 45, so further sons were a possibility.

Marriage was arranged with a young French noble lady, Yolande of Drew. She was 22.

In March of 1286 Alexander concluded business with a meeting of nobles in Edinburgh. He was determined to travel to Kinghorn in Fife to be with his young bride – no doubt he was contemplating the

urge
his p.
had n
And it

Tw
but on
stormy
on horse

After
'told him
to Inverk
him not t
the king w

If it had
from a stagg
slope. It app
enough to br
without an he

That horse
of Scotland.

Alexander III.

THE MAKING OF
THE HIGHLANDS

THE GAL GAEL

We've seen the Dal Riatan Scots, or at least the Scots elite, migrate east to merge with the Picts to form Alba. But what of the land they left behind?

How are the Highlands and Islands different?
The migration occurred because of constant attacks by the Vikings. It is likely that what happened next was that the Vikings moved in and stayed.

There is sudden appearance of a new group on the political landscape, the Gall-Ghàidheil, or Gall Gael. Gall meant 'foreigner' and was used to describe the Norse. Gall Gael was some kind of amalgam of the Norse and Gaelic.

Irish accounts at the time described them: 'they are Irish, and foster-children of the Norse, and sometimes they are even called Norsemen' and 'men who had forsaken their baptism ... for they had the customs of the Norse, and had been fostered by them'.

They first appear in the Irish records as war bands fighting in alliance with one or other Irish clan, or they may have been simple mercenaries. They are not identified as belonging to any Irish chieftain.

The experience of this Norse invasion was not uniform; in the Outer Hebrides it is likely that the takeover was overwhelming, with the emergence of the distinctively Scandinavian Kingdom of the Hebrides. In other areas the Gaelic identity, in new hybrid form, survived. Key among these areas was former Dal Riata, Argyll.

The Vikings may have been invited in as there is a record in a Scandinavian chronicle, 'Ketill Flatnose made land in Scotland, and was well received by men of rank there, for he was famous and of noble birth; they invited him to stay on his own terms.'

Such a policy made perfect sense. King Charles the Simple of France had given Normandy to the Norse specifically so they could protect his kingdom from other Vikings. Perhaps the Gaels of Argyll did a similar deal – one clan of Vikings (possibly from Sogn on the west coast of Norway) were given a permanent base and land to settle in exchange for protection. We even have a possible name for the Viking leader: Caitall Find or Kettill Flatnose.

BY THE WAY: This may or not be the same Ketill Flatnefur who was a big deal in Icelandic history. This could explain a Celtic tinge to Christianity in some parts of Iceland, including the veneration of St Columba.

The Isle of Bute seems to have been an important stronghold with its Dunagoil – Fort of the Foreigners (the same as Donegal in Ireland). The remains of the fort with vitrified walls can be visited.

This process of amalgamation between Gael and Norse was taking place over the ninth and tenth centuries while Scots and Picts were merging into Alba, though there is no suggestion that any such process happened in Strathclyde.

This is the point where Highlands and Islands culture takes a different fork and remains distinctly separate from the rest of Scotland!

It was into this emerging Gal Gael nation that a hero appears – Sumarliði – Somerled. He was dubbed Ri Airer Goidel, 'King of Argyll'. Dal Riata was gone.

THE KING OF THE ISLES

At the time of King David I's death an almost legendary Scottish–Gaelic hero emerged on the west coast. The great 'Viking Slayer' who defended Scotland against the Norwegian menace and won back the Hebrides. He became the magnificent Lord of the Isles and founded the great Highland clan: **Somairle, Somhairle, or Somhairlidh,** better known to history as Somerled.

However, it is not quite that simple.

BY THE WAY: The correct pronunciation of the man's name is 'SORLEY', not the anglicised Somerled.

GilleBride was a lord born into the Norse–Gaelic culture of the lands formerly Dal Riata – the Gal Gael. His family had lost its foothold, retreated to kinfolk in Fermanagh in the north of Ireland, but GilleBride then returned to Dal Riata to re-establish his claim; he was killed in the attempt but his son, Somerled, completed the task, taking Morvern first and expanding territory to become the Lord of Argyll.

Somerled's father may have had a genuine Dal Riatan ancestry stretching back to Kenneth MacAlpin. His mother was born Elin Sigurdsdottir.

How is it all about the Vikings?

To continue this story we need to delve briefly into the politics of the Norse kingdom. King Olaf of Man and the Hebrides, had spent time in the English court of Henry I, as had King David I. When he came to his kingship he was more inclined to contemplate relationships with Scotland and England than some of his Scandophile contemporaries.

He married one daughter to Fergus, King of Galloway and another to an upstart from the Gal Gael – Somerled.

He ruled for a remarkable forty years, and a remarkably peaceful forty years at that. His challenge eventually came from three nephews from Viking Dublin. It was told that at a parley one of them raised his axe in tribute to old King Olaf and took the king's head off with one swing. Olaf's son, Guðrøðr or Godred, returned from Norway with support, quickly defeated the three cousins and took up his inheritance.

Godred was fond of throwing his weight about and was deeply unpopular. Given Somerled's growing strength and reputation, a cabal of Norse lords approached him with the suggestion that his son, Dugald, could be installed as King of the Hebrides – Dugald was the grandson of King Olaf. A sea battle off the Isle of Man had no clear winner but did produce an agreement that the kingdom would be split between Godred and Dugald. This compromise suited no one and within two years Somerled launched a second attack and Godred fled. Somerled now had control of the whole region – Ri Innse Gael, King of the Isles.

Somerled is often described as the first 'Lord of the Isles' but that title was first used of his descendant John MacDonald of Islay 170 years later.

BY THE WAY: The title 'Lord of the Isles' still exists. The current holder is Prince Charles Windsor. He is also Duke of Rothesay (the traditional title for the heir apparent to the Scottish crown) and Earl of Carrick.

His acquired power was a threat to the King of Scots. There was a threat from incursions into his territory by one Walter FitzAllan Steward of Scotland and in retaliation Somerled launched a massive attack and met the Scottish forces in the Battle of Renfrew (near Glasgow Airport). At an early stage in the battle Somerled was struck dead (according to tradition, because of treachery). With the leader gone the conflict fizzled out.

After his death things fell apart but that was not the end of his contribution to Highland history – the Lordship of the Isles would be revived.

Somerled left three sons; the descendants of his son Aonghus went on to form the Clan McRory; the descendants of Dughall went on to form the Clan MacDougall and the descendants of Ragnald's son Donald Mor McRanald would become the Clan Donald.

The great clans were about be born and Somerled was a founding father.

BY THE WAY: Being half Gaelic and half Norse, Somerled was the perfect poster boy for Gal Gael culture. DNA analysis of his descendants concludes that there were Viking genes on his father's side, too.

THE ARRIVAL OF THE CLANS

It was in the wake of the Viking retreat from the Hebrides, after the Treaty of Perth, that the clans started to emerge. There was a lot of Norse genetics and culture left behind, but the heavy hand of the Norwegian kings of the Hebrides, Man or Dublin was gone. Somerled's 'Kingship of the Isles' had fallen apart. Local warlords were able to set up their own family 'kingdoms' in their own territories and there was much violent vying for what those territories would be.

From these 'small kings' came the 'chieftains' and their families, neighbours and associates became the highland clans. The word 'clann' literally means children but can be taken to mean 'kin'. The analogy of a family was calculated, but did not necessarily mean blood relations: many within a territory would assign themselves to a clan, sometimes taking the surname (surnames were a fairly new innovation in Gaelic society), sometimes not. Smaller clans could be co-opted under a more powerful clan's banner.

The family theme continues in regard to the clan chief. Respect and tribute were due to him from his 'children', and equally the 'children' could expect protection and support from him. But he could be replaced.

There was no rule of primogeniture – when a new chief was required, he was selected by the clan. He did have to belong to the 'first family': candidates to replace a deceased chief could be sons, brothers, nephews or cousins.

While the clans had a common Gaelic language and similar culture, they each developed along their own lines. Each invented a history to justify their claim to the land and people; in this a bit of ancient lineage was helpful.

Each clan needed their own unique origin story.

How did the clans create their own origins?
One of the most honest is the MacLeod story. Their founding father was Leod, a son of Norwegian King Olaf. After Haakon sold the Isles, Leod was left holding Lewis and Harris and parts of Skye.

Many other clans are likely to have strong Norse connections, but ancient Irish forefathers were very popular. Clans including the MacNeills, Lamonts and MacSweeneys all claimed decent from Niall of the Nine Hostages (founder of the powerful Irish O'Neil clans) as an ancestor.

The MacDonalds did have an inspiring forefather in Somerled, but that was not good enough. They traced their line back to the second-century King Conn of Ulster, or even Cuchulain, the legendary hero of the Ulster Saga.

Others like the MacKinnons and MacGregors kept it a bit more local with claims to Kenneth MacAlpin's Dal Riatan family (which had Irish roots).

The Campbells of Argyll became one of the most powerful clans of all – though their origins are somewhat tangled.

There is a claim that the name is ancient Gaelic combining the words 'cam', meaning bent or arched, and 'beul', mouth to give Cambel or 'Crooked Mouth', referring to the facial deformity of some particular ancestor. Added to this is that through marriage to the O'Duin family they are descended from Diarmid of the Boar, who was a central character in the Fenian Saga – the stories of Finn MacCool. While there may be some real character at the root of these tales, they are largely fictional.

This version gives them an ancient Irish Gaelic history; however, there are other versions. One suggests a Roman, who, after his countrymen had retired from Britain, settled among the Britons of Strath-Clyde.

More likely is the story of a Norman family, Campo Bello, who came across with William the Conqueror. A Sir Nigel de Campo Bello is recorded as attending Robert the Bruce's Parliament in 1320.

It has to be said that in later centuries the Campbells would behave more like Scotto-Norman lords than Highland chieftains. In the eighteenth century they were resolutely pro-government.

Scandinavian ancestry was distinctly out of fashion.

How did the clans progress?

The clans of the Hebrides and Highlands would develop a unique Gaelic culture steeped in story, poetry and music. It is a hugely rich tradition that was maintained as distinctly different from that Scottish culture which increasingly looked to Europe for its influences. Highland culture remained unique and consciously separate.

They also retained a strong military tradition. The clans would spend the next centuries fighting each other and the kings of Scots. They would come together in alliances and just as easily fall out. The MacDonalds would revive the Lordship of the Isles and then lose it to James IV.

During the Stuart wars many of the clans supported the Stuarts (despite centuries of enmity). Famously, they marched with Bonnie Prince Charlie in 1745. And that led to their downfall.

BRUCES AND STEWARTS

INDEPENDENCE LOST AND FOUND

Alexander III's last-ditch attempt to produce a male heir had failed when, as we have seen, he died in a fall from his horse (his young wife, Yolande, did claim to be pregnant at the time of his death but no child survived). The only option left was his granddaughter, Margaret, daughter of King Eric of Norway, known as the 'Maid of Norway'. The problem was she was only 3 years old.

In 1290 a board of Guardians of Scotland was set up. Their proposed solution for the infant princess was to get her married, or at least promised to be married – but who to marry? Why the future King of England! The problem was he was only 6 years old. This child would later be Edward II. In the meantime Scotland had to deal with his father, Edward I: Edward Longshanks, soon to be despised as 'the Hammer of the Scots'.

The deal would have meant that the King of England would be de facto the ruler of Scotland – their offspring would then claim monarchy of both countries. There was a clause that insisted the two crowns would continue to be separate, but how much that would have been honoured is debatable.

In any case, the plan was scuppered when, on a rough crossing from Norway, the child fell ill and died in Orkney.

BY THE WAY: Had Margaret lived and been married to Edward II it's hard to imagine how dreadful things might have been. He would later be described as 'the worst ever King of England'. He was almost certainly murdered by his own nobles – possibly by means of a red hot poker up the royal rectum!

Who shall be king?

There were contenders – no shortage of contenders. The Guardians were faced with the likelihood of open civil war and decided to hold a conference at which the vying claims could be examined and a winner chosen. Such an event would need a chairman: the chairman would need to have some authority to stop the whole thing collapsing into mayhem.

They chose Edward Longshanks: 'he came in a guise of a friend and ally to harass them as an enemy'.

Edward agreed to take on the task, providing the Guardians agreed that as King of England he was naturally overlord of Scotland. English kings had long treasured that idea and Edward was no doubt aware of the agreement signed by William the Lion (even though that had been annulled). Pressing his case, he did not provide any proof that he WAS overlord, he demanded that Scotland provide proof that he WAS NOT!

The Guardians came up with the slippery response that since Scotland had no king then there was no one who had the authority to answer the question.

The process was called the **'Great Cause'** – it would take two years.

Who were the contenders?

There were thirteen hats in the ring. Unfortunately, this is one of the moments where the whole dynasty and lineage comes into play and it is time to roll out the family tree. Of the Scottish candidates (Eric of Norway had put his name forward, with no good reason) all claimed direct descent from Malcolm Canmore (and thus from Kenneth MacAlpin). All but one came down the line though David I's son Henry (the one who didn't live long enough to be king).

The exception was John Comyn, whose line went back to Malcolm's brother, Donald: he was discounted.

Of the others, no fewer than six could be dismissed because they came from illegitimate children of William the Lion (he got around). Another bastard went on the same grounds.

That left four with a genuine claim. John Hastings, Lord of Abergavenny, suggested they should split Scotland up among the candidates. Floris V, Count of Holland, claimed that a document that supported his claim existed, but he didn't know where it was. That held up proceedings for a while. Neither made the final cut.

That left two, John Balliol and Robert de Brus (Remember 'name rank and number', this was Robert, 5th Lord of Annandale NOT the 'famous' Robert the Bruce!). Both families, de Bailleul and de Brus, had come over with William the Conqueror and both had come north during David I's first wave of grants of land and title. Both were decidedly Norman.

Balliol argued that he should win because of the Norman system of 'primogeniture'.

De Brus argued that under Scottish 'tanastry' he was the most fit to be king. In any case, he was closest to the recent king by kinship, being a second cousin while Balliol was third cousin. Also, he had been serving the crown for most of his life: he had actually been 'regent' of Scotland when Alexander III was underage. He had been around for a long time – he was 75.

BY THE WAY: The one candidate that gets overlooked is Edward Longshanks himself. He, like all English royals from Henry II, is descended from Malcolm Canmore through Malcolm's daughter, Matilda of Scotland.

De Brus might have thought that he would get a good result from his old friend Edward: hadn't they fought together on crusade? But Balliol did have one winning attribute – he looked malleable! For Edward that was a clincher – he looked forward to a Scottish regime that would accept his overlordship and do as they were told. John Balliol looked like the man for the job.

On 17 November 1292 Edward I declared John Balliol the winner!

How 'Toom' was his 'Tabard'?

Balliol was now John I, King of Scots. His reputation as a mere lackey to Edward earned him the nickname 'Toom Tabard' – Empty Coat. Balliol toed the line, for a while. Four years in, even he could not stand it – he renounced his homage to Edward.

Edward was not happy and sent an army north. On route they devastated Berwick-upon-Tweed and then met a Scottish army in (one of) the Battles of Dunbar.

John Balliol.

The Scots lost and many nobles were taken prisoner – many others paid homage to Edward, thus retaining their positions. John Balliol was told to abdicate – sacked!

THE FIGHTBACK

First Scottish defender in the field was Andrew de Moray, or Andrew Murray. His family was a branch of the Norman line that had been granted the region of Moray by David I.

He was one of those taken prisoner at Dunbar. Imprisoned at Chester in England, he escaped and headed home to Moray. There he

William Wallace.

raised a force in the name of King John, and took his home turf using hit and run tactics. He started clearing the English presence from the rest of the north-east.

News of his success may have helped embolden others. Another character comes into the story now – you may have heard of him? His name was William Wallace.

Braveheart?

Worldwide, William Wallace is one of the best-known persons in Scottish History. How come? It all boils down to how your story is told: Wallace's was well told. We're not talking about Mel Gibson, we're talking about Blind Harry. Blind Harry was a poet (about whom we know very little). He wrote the epic *The Actes and Deidis of the Illustre and Vallyeant Campioun Schir William Wallace* (also known as *The Wallace*). It was a hit. Aside from the Bible, it was top of the best-seller list for over a century. It casts its hero in a grand romantic, chivalric style and was written around the time the first Robin Hood ballads were popular.

Written the best part of two centuries after Wallace's death, it is no more historically accurate than the movie (it was the text the screenwriter used). Without the book, Wallace would have been a bit player – there would have been no monument and no *Braveheart*.

Not that Wallace's role should be downplayed – but he was a bit of a one-hit wonder.

He was from a family of lesser nobles – certainly not great lords, but not peasants either. Elderslie in Renfrewshire claims him as a son (there are counter-claims from Ayrshire). He may have been of Norman descent but his name could be taken as derived from the word for Welsh, which can be read as Bretonic, so he could be descended from Britons of the Kingdom of Strathclyde. A local, in fact.

His first act of rebellion was to murder the Sheriff of Lanark. Then he joined forces with William Douglas to 'liberate' Scotland's symbolic capital of Scone. This had no military significance, but it was good publicity! He slipped into the Ettrick Forest, living Robin Hood style, launching raids against the English establishment.

He met up with Andrew Murray and they engaged in the more significant action of besieging Dundee. When word came that an English army was on its way, Murray and Wallace decamped and met them at Stirling.

Stirling has always been strategically important; it is a choke point. To the west is a vast bog, impenetrable to a heavy army, while to the east the Forth is a formidable river. Stirling Bridge is the first crossing point.

BY THE WAY: The possible wooden foundations of the bridge have only recently been discovered. They are just upstream of the 'Old Stirling Bridge' (now pedestrians only).

Wallace's big day!

So began the Battle of Stirling Bridge. It is one of Scotland's most popularly celebrated battles, not least because it was actually a WIN!

The Scots were lying in wait while the English started making their way across the bridge. When there was a big enough chunk to chew, the Scots attacked. The English barging their way across made the bridge collapse. The Scots slaughtered the English on their side of the river. The English on the other side ran away: victory!

Andrew Murray either died at the battle or later from wounds. Wallace was appointed Guardian of Scotland – it must have miffed many lords that such a low-born fellow got such a title, but he was the hero of the moment and he did get knighted around this time in a ceremony in Kirk o' the Forest (Selkirk). It appears that he took his duty seriously and was making efforts to revive Scotland's export trade.

He led a successful campaign into Northumbria and Cumbria, but his next major military confrontation was on its way.

Longshank's return match

Edward Longshanks was not thrilled about the humiliating defeat at Stirling Bridge; it was time to get his 'Hammer' on. He had resolved the distraction of war in France by signing a treaty with the

French king. He moved his court to a forward position in York and summoned all the Scottish Lords to attend – those that failed to show up were marked as traitors.

He had a massive force; heavy cavalry, huge numbers of infantry (including many Welshmen) and, critically, longbowmen (maybe as many as 2,000).

The Scots were outnumbered, as they had been at Stirling Bridge. We love it when the underdog wins but it was not to be. The Scottish schiltrons (tightly packed formations with pikes sticking out like a lethal porcupine) were ravaged by overwhelming arrow-power. Once the formations started to crack, the heavy cavalry could tear them apart and the infantry finish the job. It was not a good day for the Scots.

BY THE WAY: You should cringe every time you hear, in a movie, someone ordering archers to 'FIRE'! Fire has nothing to do with it. To 'GIVE FIRE' is what you to do to make gunpowder work in a cannon or a gun. Archers 'SHOOT': the noise that an arrow makes. The command is to 'let loose' or simply 'LOOSE!'.

Wallace himself slipped away into nearby wild woods; no longer a Guardian, he was now an OUTLAW! He doesn't disappear off the scene all together. He travelled to France, and possibly even to Rome, to try to drum up support, but eventually he was captured at Robroyston (now in Glasgow) and handed over to the English and thence to London and a gory end. His various bits were sent to Berwick, Edinburgh, Stirling and Perth.

Wallace should absolutely be regarded as a Scottish hero. In his brief span in politics he was unwaveringly bent on defending Scotland from the predatory Edward I; unlike the Bruce in the early years, and he never stopped. He did, though, have only one great success (at Stirling Bridge), but that didn't slow the English down for long. It's a good story and deserves its monument.

How did the king give Scotland away (again)?

Wallace and the other protesters had raised their banners in the name of King John (Balliol), but where was he? After his abdication he was entertained for a few years in the Tower of London, then he was allowed to go to France. When he was embarking it was discovered that his luggage included the Scottish crown jewels, numerous other pricy items and a load of cash. Edward relieved him of anything significant. He ended up in one of his family's castles (remember he was pure Norman) under technical house arrest, but pretty comfortable. He made no palpable effort to get involved in Scottish affairs.

When John Balliol abdicated and the symbols of Scotland were physically stripped from his clothing, he wasn't just standing down as an individual holder of the office; he was handing the kingship of Scotland to Edward.

There was no effort to work out who should step in to the role. There was no need – the Kingship of Scotland was finished: the Kingdom of Scotland was dead!

Thereafter Edward only referred to 'the land' of Scotland'; it was just a region under England. As Wales was. As Ireland was.

THE BRUCE

You may be wondering when the big-name character is going to show up in this story. Robert de Brus, 5th Lord of Annandale, was a contender back in 1292, the one you may be thinking of is the 7th Lord of Annandale – his grandson. Your actual Robert the Bruce.

Ask any audience which kings of Scotland they've heard of? Robert the Bruce is usually first. And he will fit the bill as an 'Outlaw King', a 'Warrior King' and a bona fide 'King of Scots'.

But at this stage in the game, not so outlaw.

The de Brus family were one of Edward's first calls to defend his interests. Bruce's response was, to use the Glasgow vernacular, 'Mebbes aye, mebbes naw!' After the Falkirk disaster he had paid full homage to Edward, along with a lot of other Scottish nobles. He had his profitable properties in England to think of as the de Brus family had more land in England than they had in Annandale.

Edward came north yet again. Stirling was the last castle standing. Edward had brought some heavy artillery in the form of trebuchets, including a massive one called 'Warwolf'. It's use forced Stirling to surrender in a day.

There was no one to stop Edward now and there was nothing subtle about his approach:

> The deeds of cruelty, massacre, violence, pillage, arson, imprisoning prelates, burning down monasteries, robbing and killing monks and nuns and yet other outrages without number which he committed against our people, sparing neither age nor sex, religion nor rank, no-one could describe nor fully imagine unless he had seen them with his own eyes.

Edward was in charge and he set about reorganising this new northern part of England. He summoned a Parliament of cowed Scottish nobles to lay out the new governance of the region.

Where was Robert the Bruce?

Bruce, at this point, was considering his options. His grandfather had been runner up in the 'King of Scots' contest that John Balliol had won and then lost. Maybe Bruce, as his grandfather's heir, should have another go. He started to sound out how much support he might have, but some unreliable ears were listening to the chatter.

John Comyn was one of the most powerful nobles in Scotland: he had been one of the contenders for the crown. When he got wind of Bruce's murmurings he shopped him to Edward. To try and smooth things over and maybe organise some meaningful Scottish resistance, Bruce and Comyn arranged to meet in a church in Dumfries. They had a history of not liking each other.

We have no record of how the conversation went, but it's pretty clear that at some point Robert the Bruce 'lost the heid'. When Robert stormed out, his men came in to find Comyn on the floor, bleeding

Bruce.

profusely, and finished the job. Bruce had just killed a leading Scottish noble – and on holy ground! He was now a criminal on the run, in the eyes of Edward's state, and also a sinner in the eyes of the church.

He was in big trouble. Unless he was a king: A king could get away with this! The Kingship of Scotland WAS vacant (or maybe abolished, if Edward was to be believed).

Bruce didn't have many choices.

He went for it!

What did the bishop say?

This is a small but critical detail to all that happens next; the Scottish Church supported him. For murdering in a church, excommunication by the Pope of Rome was to be expected, but the Scottish bishops had been at the mercy of Edward's reforms and they were now told that they were subservient to the English church. They weren't happy.

The Scottish bishops, with Wishart (Bishop of Glasgow) at the front, absolved Robert the Bruce. He was bona fide in the eyes of the Lord (if only in Scotland).

How was the Bruce crowned twice?

He proceeded, with Bishop Wishart, to Scone and was made King of Scots!

Some of the movies show the Bruce being crowned by a woman. This is actually correct. The tradition was that the actual crowning was carried out by a member of the MacDuff family. Hearing of the event, Lady Isabella MacDuff, Countess of Buchan, took up the family gauntlet – although she was married to Bruce's bitter enemy, John Comyn. She made a heroic dash to get to Scone. She arrived a day late, but Bruce was happy to rerun the ceremony with Lady Isabella representing the MacDuffs – anything to prove this was all 'done richt'.

For her trouble she was one of the ladies who wound up in a cage, this one suspended from the walls of Berwick Castle.

> BY THE WAY: Ian Hamilton (the guy who stole the Stane o' Destiny from Westminster) suggests that if the 'real stane' had been secreted away and its location was known, surely it would have been brought out for this event!

Movie makers do have a problem telling the Robert the Bruce story in a couple of hours. He was no overnight sensation: at the time of his coronation it was already fourteen years since Balliol was crowned. It would be another eight years before Bruce could justifiably claim to be in control of Scotland. It would be another twenty-two years before the English would renounce their claim to be overlords.

How did it go wrong so quickly?
Things got off to a quick start when Edward acted immediately, sending an army under the Earl of Pembroke. The coronation had been in March; by June the English army were ensconced in Perth Castle.

The (over?)confident Bruce arrived with a substantial army. He demanded that Pembroke came out from behind the walls and face him in open battle. Pembroke, reasonably, said it was a bit late in the day, but he would come out and play tomorrow. What Bruce didn't know or understand was that the English were campaigning under the 'Dragon Banner'. This meant that all the general rules of chivalry were suspended; cheating was allowed and no mercy would be shown. It does sound like fiction, but it was real enough as Bruce was about to find out.

He naively took the earl at his word and moved to camp for the night at nearby Methven. The Scots had got all their gear off and settled down for the night. Either at dusk or just before dawn the English attacked, catching the Scots with their chain mail down. It wasn't a battle, it was slaughter. Bruce was thrown from his horse several times. Among the chaos a small band of brothers formed up around the king and, by the skin of their teeth, forced their way off the field and ran. Many supporters were killed or carted off to be executed later (Dragon Banner, remember).

It was a disaster! Bruce's kingship was nearly over before the starting whistle had gone in the very first match!

And it didn't get better any time soon. Bruce's wife, sisters and daughter had been sent away north to stay out of harm's way, to Kildrummy Castle in Aberdeenshire. In September an English force attacked Kildrummy. Bruce's youngest brother, Nigel, was captured and sent for public execution in Berwick, along with several others. The ladies had managed to get away but were captured a few days later (along with Lady Isabella) and sent to their various fates.

How did Bruce disappear!

No one knows for sure where he spent the winter of 1306. Some have suggested Orkney, or even Norway. The Hebrides or the north of Ireland are more likely. The 'Bruce and the Spider story' is associated with Rathlin Island (just off the north Irish coast), but several other caves claim the tale.

BY THE WAY: The well-known story tells that Bruce watches a spider try to cast its web only to fail again and again. On the seventh go it succeeds and Bruce is inspired to keep trying and heads back to Scotland. The tale is very probably a literary invention (first written in print by Walter Scott), but it is a nice wee fable that illustrates the hopelessness of his situation and the resolve it took not to give up. You never know, it might have happened.

Spider or not, Bruce returned in February 1307. He and his brother, Edward, landed at Turnberry, while his brothers, Thomas and Alexander, landed a second force farther south in Loch Ryan. The Thomas and Alexander campaign quickly came to grief: both were captured and murdered.

After a skirmish in Glen Trool, Bruce got to face the Earl of Pembroke (the guy that humiliated him at Methven) at Loudon Hill. Bruce wasn't going to be fooled twice. He chose his ground and made his preparations. He enlisted the landscape in the form of a bog. He got the spades out.

Trenches blocked the ground around the bog, forcing Pembroke's cavalry to charge along a narrow path. They ran headlong into Bruce's spearmen. Bruce was learning. Although this was a victory, open battle was something Bruce would avoid for the next few years.

How should you not let Bruce into your castle?

He headed north with a new tactic. He had enough experience of English tactics (having fought on the English side often enough) to use this knowledge to his advantage.

The Norman English were great fans of castles, going right back to William the Conqueror's mottes and baileys. The Edwards, father and son, had installed their own men or dependable Scots in castles the length and breadth of Scotland. These would show an ever-present threat to the locals and maintain a foothold that would provide shelter and support in the event of the English army arriving on campaign. These forays usually happened in the summer – in the winter the widely scattered castles were manned by fairly small garrisons. Bruce saw an opportunity.

He started attacking castles; Inverlochy, Urquhart, Inverness and Nairn. He took the castles but he had nowhere near the manpower to actually hold and occupy them. What he could do was 'break' them (that is the technical term): he would destroy walls and gates, he would set fire to them. Anything to render them uninhabitable or at least undefendable. Destroying castles made sense strategically, but also psychologically. Seeing the English threat literally going up in smoke was good for engendering hope that Scotland could win. More and more people were starting to believe in Bruce.

How was Bruce coming for Comyn?
Next he turned into Aberdeenshire. More castles; Duffus, Balvenie, Tarradale and eventually Inverness. This attack on the north-east was no accident. Very often any Scottish initiative is under more threat from division within Scotland than anything coming over the border. Bruce's biggest threat were the Comyn family: Bruces and Comyns had long been bitter rivals. Robert Bruce hadn't helped by murdering John Comyn in Dumfries. The Comyns were the Earls of Buchan and Badenoch and the north-east was their power base.

The Comyns came to battle at Barra Hill near Inverurie. Facing Bruce was John Comyn, 3rd Earl of Buchan (cousin to the Dumfries John Comyn). The Comyn forces and allies may have been encouraged by news that Bruce was seriously ill, but Bruce rose from his sickbed and appeared on the battlefield. It was a bloody victory for the king.

Brother Edward followed up by a spot of 'harrying'; devastating property, stores and livestock across Buchan. Slains Castle, Rattray Castle and Dundarg Castle, then the English-held Fyvie Castle were all 'broken'. The big prize of Aberdeen Castle also fell.

Two years into this campaign he was pretty much in control of everything north of the Tay. In March 1309 he held his first Parliament in Saint Andrews. From there it was a slow process of knocking out the big English-held castles at Linlithgow, Dumbarton and Perth.

1314 and all that
By 1314 it had been eight years of endless bloody grind since his coronation. There were only a couple of big targets left.

Roxburgh was important. It fell in March of that year.

Edinburgh, you might think, would be a big one. If you're one of the 1.7 million annual visitors you might look over the cliffs at the west end of the castle and reckon them to be a perfect defence. Not so. Bruce's men, under Thomas Randolph, 1st Earl of Moray, climbed up at night and took the castle by surprise. Bruce subsequently did a lot of damage, as was his usual way.

BY THE WAY: Edinburgh Castle may look pretty impressive but it has been 'taken' no fewer than SIX times in its history.

That left only one castle standing – Stirling. Robert's brother, Edward Bruce, was taking care of that offensive: he laid siege. It is easy to suspect that Edward was something of an impetuous character. Sitting around in a muddy Stirlingshire field waiting for the English garrison to starve was not his style.

He made a deal with the Governor, Philip de Mowbray, that if the castle was not relieved by Mid-Summer's Day the castle would be handed over with no further waste of Edward's valuable time. Apparently big brother Robert was not happy about the deal; the fall of the castle was only a matter of time, whereas a set deadline might have another consequence. Robert was right.

Where was the King of England?

Meantime in England, Edward II was having enough trouble at home; he had been deeply unpopular from the start. His shameless promotion of his boyfriend, Piers Gavestan, had enraged many nobles. Since Edward was kept busy in England, he had let matters in Scotland slide. Bruce's rise from scruffy outlaw to patent ruler of Scotland had gone unchallenged.

The 'Stirling Challenge' was an opportunity. A major military victory might do wonders to bolster his standing among his subjects, so he assembled an army. Some key nobles refused to co-operate but he did manage to gather a MASSIVE force.

Figures are unreliable; most quoted is 3,000 cavalry, 13,000 infantry plus Welsh archers. Some put it higher.

The Scottish forces totalled around 7,000 men. The Scots included nobles and men from the north-east and the south-west and from the centre; there were Highlanders and Borderers – it was the first ever truly SCOTTISH army.

Edward headed for Stirling to get there by the deadline of 24 June. Bruce, despite his long-term avoidance of open battles, had no choice but to face him.

How did the battle go?

There are many people who delight in following detailed battle plans. There are precise accounts available of many of the battles mentioned in this book, you are welcome to seek them out. We have largely left that to others, but Bannockburn is a particularly interesting battle. It was unusual in that, unlike most battles that were over in a matter of hours, it took two days. It is worth a little explanation.

Most of Bruce's were men were foot soldiers armed with a pike (a spear about 12ft long), plus a knife or club for mopping up anyone unfortunate enough to be on the ground. They were simply armed but they were NOT untrained. They were formed into tightly packed 'schiltrons'. Schiltrons had been a disaster at Falkirk; the archers broke them up.

Bruce's schiltrons had a new innovation – they could move! Shifting such a tight formation of very spiky men could easily degenerate into a lethal shambles. At Bannockburn, thanks to a bit of training, it worked. Schiltrons were no longer a defensive block, they were (very slow) 'attack dogs'.

There were four; under Edward Bruce, James Douglas, Thomas Randolph and Robert himself. One on the main road, one on either side, and another in reserve. And Bruce had also had his spades out.

He had, however, been careless enough to leave a big space open on the left – from Edward's point of view.

Edward II must have been feeling pretty good with that huge array of experienced heavy knights behind him, compared to the much smaller Scottish rabble he could see before him. He could have stopped and rested his men; they had just marched from Berwick, but this outlaw wasn't going to take long. He paused.

BY THE WAY: The movies usually portray war horses as huge stomping, snorting beasts. A recent study of the remains of over 2,000 horses' remains reveals that the majority of Medieval horse were less than 4.2 hands high, 4ft 10in at the shoulder. That is the upper end of the height range for a modern highland pony. A modern thoroughbred is up to 17 hands (5ft 8in), while Clydesdales go to 18 hands (6ft). Mind you, if a horse is coming at you full pelt with a big guy in armour swinging a sword or a mace, you don't get out a tape measure!

How was there a 'single combat' moment?

Now comes one of those wonderful moments of pure theatre that you might expect was a movie invention, but there is plenty of evidence that it did take place.

The two armies were facing each other. A young English knight, Henry de Bohun, spotted the Bruce himself out in front of his troops. He might have been giving the pre-battle speech (loved by movies), if more than a handful of the men could have heard him. Bruce was not even kitted up for battle, or even on his warhorse.

De Bohun saw the opportunity to end the battle now and write himself into history as an English hero. He snapped down his visor, kicked his heels into his horse, lowered his lance and CHARGED!

Nobody had much chance to react. It could be critical if the king was taken out before the battle started. Bruce, the seasoned warrior, watched the knight hurtling towards him. At the last minute, Bruce's pony did a neat 'body swerve', the lance missed. The knight's momentum carried him on, past the Bruce. The Bruce swung his battleaxe on to Bohun's head, crashing through his helmet and his skull and 'cleaving him to the neck'. Bruce complained he had broken a good axe.

It was a perfect moment – you couldn't make this stuff up. In full view of his troops the king, without armour, wielding a simple axe, had destroyed a fully armoured, fully trained English knight. Better than any speech he could have made. It was the perfect metaphor!

Bruce and Bohun.

If it was the ideal moral boost for the Scots, it was the opposite for the English.

Edward had his knights, but the only thing that knights can do is charge; Edward ordered 'CHARGE!' That's when they found out about the Scots' spade work. The pits were deep enough to trip the horse and fling the rider – and they were lined with pointed sticks – nobody who fell was getting back up. The track they were forced into was headlong into the Scottish schiltrons, which had been the plan. Infantry is supposed to panic and turn and run, easy meat for armoured men. Bruce's men didn't. They held firm.

Horses are not particularly keen on running into a hedge of spears. For a man with a 12ft-long spear, a horse is pretty hard to miss (particularly if it's running straight at you). An armoured knight on the ground is now the 'easy meat'. So long as the formation does not break, then 'pikes beat horses'. The Scottish formations did not break.

Day one was done with the Scots ahead.

Time to reposition for tomorrow. Bruce's careless neglect of that empty ground to Edward's left had not gone unnoticed. The space was the 'New Park', a hunting ground for kings visiting Stirling. It was 'mixed ground' on the banks of the River Forth, woods and marsh, crossed by two burns. The English crossed the burn and took up position to attack the Scottish flank, avoiding the disastrous pits. Clever!

Clever? Instead of the open road to Berwick behind them, they now had the mighty River Forth. They were flanked on one side by the Bannockburn and the Pellstream burn (no great obstacle to light foot soldiers, but a disaster for heavy knights). They had woodland to their right, but they were focused on the Scots arrayed in front of them. The Scots schiltrons had wheeled to face them.

The Scots knelt in prayer. For a moment Edward thought they were kneeling to him seeking forgiveness. He was assured that they were asking God for forgiveness for what they were about to do.

The neat English formations of yesterday were gone. It was knights out front and everyone else in a ragged line behind. Edward gave the only order he had, 'CHARGE!' The knights went headlong into Edward Bruce's schiltron. Which did not break.

Out of the ominous woods on their right came the Randolph and Douglas schiltrons, straight into their flank.

How were the archers not there?

Where were the archers that had done so much damage at Falkirk? In the wrong place to start with. They had tried shooting over the heads of their cavalry, but were hitting their own nobles and were told to desist. They moved to a position where they could get a clean shot – but the Scots were prepared. Bruce only had a few light horsemen (useless against heavy knights) and they were in reserve, but they now swept in on the archers – 'horses beat archers'. And took them out!

'On them!'

The chant of the Scots spearmen was 'ON THEM! ON THEM!'. Once the momentum of the charge was spent the knights were helpless against the slow but relentless push of the spears. They were being driven back into their own infantry.

Then by a masterstroke, or plain luck, the banners of Bruce's 'second army' appeared on the hill top. There was no 'second army'. There might have been a party of unruly Highlanders held in reserve, but the popular story is that these were the rude servants and women from the Scottish camp, the 'small folk', with makeshift flags making their own statement.

The second army wasn't needed: the English were beaten. It was utter mayhem; infantry were trodden under foot by panicking cavalry – the only way out was back the way they had come. The modest stream, the Bannock burn, was now a death trap. The Scots pushed on!

The Earl of Pembroke grabbed King Edward (who to be fair had fought bravely) and dragged him off the field. With a small bunch of nobles, he headed for the castle, where he was turned away. His presence would have meant another lengthy siege and this time there would be no prospect of a relief force. Edward made it away eventually, back to England.

Huge numbers of English nobles were dead and many foot soldiers were dispatched where they lay. Many more were slaughtered in the ragged retreat to the border.

'Freedom!'

It was an overwhelming victory for Robert I and for Scotland, and it is huge in the Scottish consciousness to this day. Deservedly so, as it was one of the greatest battles ever fought in the name of Scotland. Certainly the greatest victory. Celebrated in culture through songs including 'Scots Whae Hae' by Robert Burns (formerly Scotland's unofficial national anthem) and 'Flower of Scotland' by Roy Williamson (currently Scotland's unofficial national anthem).

We haven't forgotten!

Robert de Brus had lived through the occupation of Scotland under Edward I. From 24 June 1314 he could truly say he was ruler of Scotland. From Edward's invitation to judge the 'Great Cause' it had taken twenty-two years.

The War of Independence was won.

How was Edward not satisfied?

Edward II's great expedition was a humiliating failure, but he still wouldn't let it go: he would not renounce his claim to be overlord of Scotland. In reality there was not much he could do about it; he had plenty of trouble at home and there was no way he could raise another army any time soon. Yet his claim lingered as a potential future threat.

In 1320 the nobles of Scotland did something about it. They wrote a letter.

How is the Declaration of Arbroath important?

The Declaration of Arbroath is a letter that was sent to the Pope. It is only a thousand words long but it contains some very interesting stuff. It is undoubtedly one of the most significant documents in Scottish history.

It includes the stirring words ...

as long as a hundred of us remain alive, never will we on any conditions be subjected to the lordship of the English.

It is in truth not for glory, nor riches, nor honours that we are fighting, but for freedom alone, which no honest man gives up but with life itself.

A true statement of the nation!

But it contains a lot more than that.

Pope John XXII had supported the English. In 1319 he had excommunicated King Robert (again) along with several Scottish bishops, for not attending a papal court. The declaration was signed by eight earls and thirty-one barons on behalf of 'the whole community of the realm of Scotland'. It is written in a very polite and respectful tone and is a plea to the Pope to use his influence to force England to recognise Robert Bruce as King of Scots.

It contains a fascinating history of the Scots nation, tracing its ancestry back to ancient Scythia, which is the Dalriatan–Irish origin story. It claims an ancient royal lineage; 'In their kingdom there have reigned one hundred and thirteen kings of their own royal stock, the line unbroken by a single foreigner,' tracing the royal line back to the ancient Irish kings.

Of the Scottish nation it says, 'The Britons it first drove out, the Picts it utterly destroyed.' This is remarkable as the majority of the people calling themselves Scottish at this time were ethnically Pictish or Bretonic – this Dal Riatan–Scots version of history obliterates their entire stories.

It then launches into a full tirade against Edward Longshanks:

he came in a guise of a friend and ally to harass them as an enemy. The deeds of cruelty, massacre, violence, pillage, arson, imprisoning prelates, burning down monasteries, robbing and killing monks and nuns and yet other outrages without number which he committed against our people, sparing neither age nor sex, religion nor rank, no-one could describe nor fully imagine unless he had seen them with his own eyes.

It warns the Pope to be aware of English propaganda and urges him not to put 'too much faith in the tales the English tell'.

It finishes with an unveiled threat that if their plea was not answered, not only would there be war, but that the Pope should get the blame:

then the slaughter of bodies, the perdition of souls, and all the other misfortunes that will follow, inflicted by them on us and by us on them, will, we believe, be surely laid by the Most High to your charge.

It does get on to the business of recognising Robert the Bruce as king ...

But from these countless evils we have been set free, by the help of Him who though He afflicts yet heals and restores, by our most tireless prince, King and lord, the lord Robert.

How is the Declaration REALLY important?
It also includes a truly remarkable clause ...

Yet if he should give up what he has begun, seeking to make us or our kingdom subject, to the King of England or the English, we should exert ourselves at once to drive him out as our enemy.

It is a plain statement that if the king did not live up to expectations then he would be REMOVED! This is a far cry from the 'Divine Right of Kings', which would be invoked by Bruce's descendants in the centuries to come. This is a bold assertion that the king rules by consent of his subjects (or at least the noble ones).

It is, in fact a declaration of a 'constitutional monarchy'. It is the first such sentiment in the whole of Europe.

In essence the Declaration of Arbroath is not simply a plea to recognise a king, it is a plea to recognise a NATION.

Scotland had arrived in Europe!

How did PEACE happen?
When Edward II refused to back down he was gruesomely despatched by his own nobles. His son was crowned Edward III.

In 1324, a full decade after Bannockburn, the Bruce signed 'The Treaty of Edinburgh-Northampton'. It includes the words, 'it is treated and accorded that the said kings, their heirs and successors, shall be good friends and loyal allies …'

England and Scotland, good friends and loyal allies? 'Aye, right!', as they say in Glasgow.

What of the Bruce and his Braveheart?

His life work completed, within a year of signing the treaty he was dead. One English writer claimed he died of leprosy, but there is nothing to support this – syphilis is more likely.

So where is the great tomb celebrating this truly remarkable king? Where is he buried?

The answer is the question, 'Which bit?'

The authors go into this story in much greater length in a previous book, *Scottish History: Strange but True*. His body was buried in Dunfermline Abbey. The tomb was lost and then rediscovered in 1817. His internal organs were preserved and kept in St Serf's Chapel in Dumbarton, while his heart is in Melrose Abbey.

The heart has its own remarkable tale.

It had long been Bruce's vow to go on crusade to the Holy Land to regain the good graces of the Pope, if not the Deity himself. He had run out of time. But if he couldn't go, his heart could.

The heart was encased in a silver casket. The casket was entrusted to Sir James Douglas, who wore it around his neck. The heart was to be taken to the Church of Holy Sepulchre in Jerusalem and Bruce's vow would be deemed fulfilled, so Douglas went off to find a crusade. None were leaving from England or France, so he made his way to Spain, where it was rumoured that King Alfonso XI was planning to march east. It turned out he was battling the Moorish territory of Grenada, which was right on the Spanish border. In 1330 Douglas and his fellow Scots followed Alfonso into the Battle of Teba.

Pursuing fleeing Muslim cavalry, Douglas is said to have hurled the casket before him yelling, 'Now pass thou onward before us, as thou wert wont, and I will follow thee or die.' The Muslims, however, turned and the Scots were in retreat. Douglas was trying to withdraw when he saw his companion, Sir William de St Clair of

Rosslyn, surrounded by Moorish warriors. Ignoring the odds against him, he moved in with his men to rescue his friend, but it was too late – Douglas and most of his men were killed. His body and Bruce's casket were later recovered from the battlefield. Bruce's heart was sent back to Scotland, where it was buried, as the king had requested, in Melrose Abbey. It hadn't got within 2,000 miles of Jerusalem.

THIS was the 'Brave Heart'. The heart that made the journey and went into battle without its owner. Nothing to do with Wallace.

What did he look like?

All the semi-realistic portraits used in this book so far are lies! They are inventions created by artists centuries after the fact, but we do have a possibly realistic image. A cast of the skull discovered in Dunfermline Abbey was handed over to twenty-first-century scientists. Using up to date 'forensic reconstruction technology' they created a bust of what Bruce may actually have looked like.

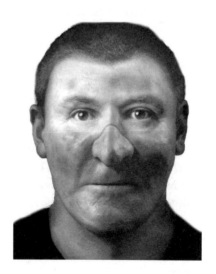

Bruce Recon.

THE EARLY STEWARTS

After Robert the Bruce's son, David II, had an innings the kingship passed to a family who would hold it for 343 years or 395 years – the Stewarts (originally the FitzAllans). To start their story in Scotland we need to backtrack slightly to David I.

How were the FitzAllans 'British'?

It is not at all uncommon for folk in positions of power to rewrite their family history according to what is most politically convenient and the Stewarts were no exception. Scottish historian Hector Boece, writing in the early sixteenth century, claimed they were descended from Banquo, who may be familiar thanks to Shakespeare's Scottish play. This would have given a convenient ancient Scottish (indeed, Pictish) lineage, but it is bunkum. They were not Scottish, but they may have been British!

The Stewarts' forebears, the FitzAlans, arrived in Scotland as part of King David I's Normanisation of Scotland, around 1136. But they were not Normans! They were from Brittany; Bretons or British, in fact.

When the family first became established in England they were given strongholds in Shropshire overseeing the Welsh border. Many of the natives would have spoken Bretonic (in the form we now call Welsh). It made sense to send in a knight who, while thoroughly in tune with the Norman mission, had grown up familiar with Bretonic culture and language.

Similarly, in Scotland it made sense to place the Bretonic FitzAlans in Renfrewshire – part of the previously powerful Bretonic/British Kingdom of Strathclyde. Who better to understand (and destroy) the vestiges of that culture? The FitzAlans were certainly involved in the military campaigns against the final Scottish Bretonic stronghold, the Kingdom of Galloway.

The first of the family to come from France was Alan FitzFlaad, sometime after the conquest. He became tangled up in the war between the impressive Queen Matilda and her cousin Stephen, both heirs of William the Bastard (he is better known as 'the Conqueror' but 'the Bastard' does have a ring to it).

The name changed to FitzAllan with the next generation. The oldest boy, Jordan, returned to order the affairs in Brittany; William took the English holdings in Shropshire; Walter, the youngest, took the less-assured course of following King David north.

How did Walter FitzAllan get more than a job for life?

He must have been trusted, as he was appointed 'Steward' to the king. The role of king's organiser already existed, the title was new; the family had fulfilled a similar role for the Lords of Brittany. He was rewarded with lands mostly around Renfrewshire where he founded Paisley Abbey, but later settled on Dundonald, near Kilmarnock, as his home castle.

As a soldier he was probably involved in the campaigns against Fergus, King of Galloway. He found himself on the front line when Somerled, Lord of the Isles, invaded Scotland, launching an attack on Paisley, Walter's territory. At no point, however, does he make the headlines as a commander.

Walter dutifully served David and his successor, Malcolm IV, and his successor, William I. He seems to have done a good job as the post was made hereditary. So began the line of FitzAllan – the stewards.

Walter FitzAllan to Allan FitzWalter to Alexander FitzAllan to Stewart

We say FitzAllan but, since 'Fitz' is equivalent to 'Mac' or 'Son of', things switched around so Walter FitzAlan's son became known as Alan FitzWalter. Inheriting the role of steward, he served William the Lion and may have gone on crusade with Richard the Lionheart.

He was followed by another Walter, then an Alexander, for a change. The title of steward had by now morphed into the surname Stewart. This Alexander Stewart had a military career, defeating the Vikings at the Battle of Largs (with the help of the Scottish weather) on behalf of King Alexander III.

In the period leading up to the War of Independence he was one of the vacillating vassals, supporting Edward Longshanks when convenient, but, by and large, he backed Robert Bruce, who turned out to be the winning horse in the end.

How did the Stewarts 'start with a lass'?

Marjorie was the only child of Robert Bruce's first wife, Isabella. She was 10 years old in 1306 when her father was crowned king, but there was ten years of conflict to go before Scotland was secured at Bannockburn. Marjorie was quickly caught up in it.

After the disastrous Battle of Methven, Bruce sent Marjorie, her stepmother, Elizabeth De Burgh, and her two aunts north for

Maid of Norway.

safekeeping. This was not to be; the party was captured and handed over to the English. The stepmother got off pretty lightly (Edward wanted the support of the father, the Earl of Ulster). Aunt Mary was imprisoned in a cage hung from the walls of Roxburgh Castle alongside Lady Isabella MacDuff. Marjorie narrowly missed a similar fate. A cage was built in the Tower of London for the young girl, but Edward relented and she was sent to a nunnery.

After Bannockburn an exchange was arranged and she was sent north to freedom. King Robert sent an official to greet her at the border and that's where it all started – the official was the Sixth High Steward of Scotland (son of James FitzAlan/Stewart). We have no record of whether the fateful encounter led to any semblance of a romance or if Walter was simply rewarded for services rendered, but the two were married shortly afterwards.

In due course she was expecting a child. Late in the pregnancy, she was riding near Paisley when she was thrown from her horse – she gave birth to a premature son.

Many years later James V, reflecting on his family's progress, pointed out that, 'It started with a lass ...' This 19-year-old girl was that lass. The child would (eventually) become Robert II of Scotland. The title 'Steward of Scotland' would become the family name Stewart (and then Stuart). The dynasty began that lasted for 343 years and 'ended with a lass' – Queen Anne. They held the crown of England through some turbulent times (if you count James VIII as Kings of Scots, that would make it 395 years).

Marjorie was to see none of it. She died soon after the birth and it would be another fifty-five years before the boy became Robert II.

BY THE WAY: James V's deathbed quote was, 'It started wi' a lass and it'll gang wi' a lass!' He was wrong and right. He was thinking of his baby daughter, Mary, but her life was not the end of the Stewarts but the beginning of the Stuarts and the tenure of the English throne. That could be said to end with Queen Anne – a lass. But if you count James VIII he was wrong all together!

Aye, Naw, Aye, Naw, Aye!

As the only child of Robert Bruce and his first wife Isabella (Isabella died at 19, about the same age as her daughter), Marjorie stood in line for the throne. And consequently her son! But before the boy was born it was decided that Robert Bruce's brother, Edward, should get the crown. So Marjorie's Robert was out.

Edward Bruce then decided that since his big brother was King of Scots he should be King of Ireland; he spent three bloody years trying to make it so. After some early success the whole adventure turned sour. Edward was killed in battle and his head sent off to Edward II in England. Robert the Steward was back in line.

Robert Bruce, after a respectable six years' widowhood, married Elizabeth de Burgh, daughter of the Anglo-Norman Earl of Ulster. Eventually they had a son, David, who displaced Robert the Steward from the succession – again.

David duly became David II and held the throne of Scotland for forty-two turbulent years

Independence – the sequel

Many people are aware of the 'War of Scottish Independence' thanks to such high-profile celebrities as William Wallace and Robert the Bruce. Not so much is said about the SECOND War of Scottish Independence. There are no movies. This was an untidy affair that dragged on for twenty-five years and, at times, looked like overturning everything that Bannockburn had achieved, taking up most of David II's reign.

It started with Edward Balliol, son of John Balliol who Robert Bruce had replaced. He claimed his father's place as sovereign and marched north, sparking a civil war as some Scottish nobles stuck with David and the Bruce family, while others aligned with the young Balliol. After some initial success, Balliol had himself crowned and Scotland (briefly and tenuously) had a King Edward (Balliol). This King Edward immediately pledged allegiance to King Edward in England (the English Edward was now the Edward III), in much the same way as his father had aligned with Edward I.

Edward Balliol was forced to flee, but returned the following year with more open support from Edward of England. Resuming his claimed kingship, Balliol gifted not just Berwick-upon-Tweed, but much of southern Scotland, including Edinburgh, to the English.

By the winter of 1333 things were looking bad for the Bruce faction. Many Scottish strongholds were in the hands of Balliol supporters. David slipped away from his refuge in Dumbarton and headed for France. The Auld Alliance was in play; ironic perhaps, since it was John Balliol who had signed it in the first place.

How did the king try to give Scotland away, again?

Fortunes rattled backward and forward until 1341, when David felt safe enough to come back to Scotland. The war continued until David was captured at a battle near Durham and spent the next decade as a prisoner in England. He was eventually released for the eye-watering

David II and Edward III.

sum of 100,000 marks! This was to be paid in instalments. When David couldn't meet his obligations, he apparently tried to barter Scotland's crown, offering it to King Edward's family (after his own death, of course). This would never have been accepted in Scotland and nothing came of it.

STEWART AT LAST

Despite being married for thirty-four years to the daughter of Edward II of England (yes, the guy who lost Bannockburn) and also remarrying after her death, David II died childless.

Finally, Robert Stewart, son of Walter and Marjorie, was back in line again. He was crowned King of Scots on 26 March 1371 at the age of 55. The Stewart monarchy had begun!

Robert was more concerned with buttressing the Stewart family fortunes than with cross-border affairs. The most remembered battle of his reign (largely because of the lengthy ballad written about it) was Otterburn. This was the one Scottish victory in a campaign instigated by Robert's eldest son, John. Robert spent more of his later years in conflict with his own offspring than with anyone else. He lived to the remarkable age of 74, when he was succeeded by John.

Not-King John and Not-King Robert

There is no King John II. John chose to be crowned Robert III, perhaps to reinforce his connection to the now legendary (thanks to the book *The Brus* by John Barbour, commissioned by his father) Robert the Bruce. This gets confusing as there already was a Robert Stewart – his younger brother. And it is ironic that this not-king Robert was actually the real power in Scotland. As Duke of Albany, he effectively ruled the land through his position as Lieutenant of Scotland.

Robert III's son, David, tried to stand up to his uncle but he was captured and imprisoned in Falkland Palace, where he mysteriously died. His uncle was suspected of foul deeds but a court found that the death was 'by providence and not otherwise'.

Not surprisingly, his younger brother, James, was feeling vulnerable. After hiding out among the gannets on the Bass Rock, he took the familiar royal course of fleeing to France; he didn't make it: his ship was intercepted by English pirates and he found himself in the equally familiar position for Scottish royalty, a prisoner of the English king. It would be eighteen years before he saw Scotland again.

Within a couple of months of his capture his father died and, at the age of 11, he was King of Scots – but without the trip to Scone and the official ceremony.

EARLY JAMES

We now have five Jameses in a row, before a wee break with a Mary. They do share a few things in common – they all lived short lives and had bizarre deaths – being a Scottish monarch was definitely not good for your health. All these early deaths meant that Scotland was plagued by one 'child monarch' after another, resulting in extended periods when the country was ruled by regents. Sometimes the king-mother held the post for a time, otherwise one Scottish noble or another got the job.

The position was much sought after as it granted the actual power to rule the kingdom. Inevitably there was conflict and even warfare over the job. Actual possession of the physical person of the king-to-be was important, with the result that the infant monarchs often found themselves as prisoners in their own castles or – someone else's.

Over this period there are only occasional 'head-to-heads' with the English, although these were sometimes fatal. That does not mean there was peace: there was almost ceaseless conflict within

James I.

Scotland; Stewarts versus Stewarts, Stewarts versus other nobles, Stewarts against the Highlanders, Stewarts against the Borderers. In terms of Scotland's place in the world, not much changes.

James I – the one that died in a sewer

At last we had a King James, with seven more to follow. It was hardly his father's intention to give the kingdom a new line of names – his older sons were predictably Robert, who died young, and David, almost certainly murdered.

> BY THE WAY: James was a forename used repeatedly by the FitzAlan/Stewards from a family association with St James the Greater, celebrated at Santiago de Compostela. It was virtually unknown as a Christian name in Scotland before. Even then James wasn't front and centre. Most eldest sons were named Alan or Walter. We might have had a succession of King Walters. The Walterite Rebellions, perhaps.

James I is, perhaps, best known for being stabbed in a sewer, which he had previously blocked to stop losing his balls. That's certainly how it ended. His reign's beginning was hardly auspicious. He was still a child and a prisoner of the English. It would be eighteen years before he made it to Scone for his coronation.

Opinion has been divided as to what to make of him. On the one hand he was well educated and cultured (thanks to the English court), an accomplished musician and a poet. He was a keen sportsman across a range of disciplines – including tennis – and it was said that he would offer to wrestle any man of any size. By and large he avoided committing the country to international wars; his most open military endeavours were against the Highlands.

On the other hand, he was seen as a tyrant grabbing power and lands into his own hands, squeezing every shilling he could from his subjects. He certainly failed to keep enough of the powerful Scottish nobles on his team. His perpetual, deadly struggles were, just like his father and grandfather, with his own family.

How did he get on as a prisoner of the English?

James I's years of imprisonment were not overly harsh. While he did spend some time in the Tower of London, much of his stay was in royal residences rather than dungeons. He was pretty much treated as a guest and friend to King Henry IV and then Henry V. His companion for part of this time was his cousin, Murdoch.

James became a trusted commander in Henry V's army in France. This led to the situation where he was against Scottish forces who's service, invoked under the Auld Alliance, saw them fighting on the side of the French Dauphin.

Meantime, in Scotland his Uncle Robert, Duke of Albany, the very man James had fled from, was in command. He was in no hurry to organise a ransom for James. The exchange of Cousin Murdoch (who happened to be Uncle Robert's son) was much higher on the agenda than the return of the king, so Murdoch saw Scotland nine years before James.

In 1424, after Henry V's death, the English regency was keen to offload their Scottish guest and he was returned to Scotland (albeit for a ransom). At last James was crowned.

How did James get revenge?

James had not forgotten the actions of Uncle Robert. Revenge was due! Unfortunately, Robert had died peacefully. Cousin Murdoch (the one who was James's companion in London) was now Duke of Albany. The axe was to fall, literally, on him and his whole family. Within a year Murdoch, his brother Duncan and his sons, Walter, Alexander and Duncan were arrested and duly beheaded in front of Stirling Castle.

James spent four years trying to curb the threat from the Gaelic Highlanders under the third Lord of the Isles. Nothing conclusive was achieved and financial support for the campaigns petered out.

The death of Murdoch and family wasn't popular with everyone. James then proceeded to alienate his Uncle Walter, the Earl of Atholl, and his family (Walter had previously been an ally). When James attended a General Council in Perth, Walter's territory, his hosts were in on the plot.

How did the sewer death happen?

James's lifetime love of sports was to be his undoing. Playing tennis, he had been annoyed at losing balls down a drain and so had ordered it to be blocked off so he could retrieve them. When a party of the disgruntled nobles (about thirty of them) were let into the building, James had nowhere to hide but in that very drain. Cornered, he was stabbed repeatedly and bled to death in the sewer.

The attackers were remiss in failing to also murder the queen, Joan, which had been the plan: although injured, she escaped. This may have been crucial. She lived as a rallying point for those who would oppose the conspirators and for the defence of her children, including the next James.

James II – the one that went with a bang

Queen Joan escaped with her life and her son! She whisked him off to Holyrood Abbey, where he was crowned king at the age of 6. She tried to keep control of the boy, but it was not to be. Lords Livingston and Crichton grabbed the boy and his mother and held them in Stirling Castle.

James II managed to avoid war with his uncles and brothers – he went to war with his cousins instead – the Douglases.

How was the dinner 'Black'?

Livingstone and Crichton were very wary of the power of the Douglas family. Archibald Douglas had married into the royal line, giving his two sons a claim to the throne; they could be a threat.

The two boys, William and David, were invited to a play date with the boy king at Edinburgh Castle. They were there for a fortnight. After dinner one evening the severed head of a black bull was brought in on a platter and ceremoniously placed on the table – this was not a good sign! Beware Scots bearing bull's heads.

The two Douglas boys were 'tried', found guilty, hauled outside and beheaded in the courtyard. The young king pleaded for their lives. He was 10 years old.

As soon as he came of age, James wasted no time in ousting his former prison masters, Livingstone and Crichton. Conflict with

James II.

the Douglases took a bit more effort. In 1542 he invited William Douglas to parley at Stirling Castle, where Douglas was accused of making an alliance with MacDonald, Lord of the Isles. The conversation appears to have got a little heated. James drew a dagger and stabbed the Douglas in the neck; then stabbed him again, and again. The king's officials then joined the party, at least one of them with an axe. The mutilated body was thrown from the window.

This did not solve the Douglas problem. James's war against his own nobles dragged on for another three years.

Once again a Stewart king was confounded by internal strife rather than through making a noise on a wider stage. He did make one move against the 'Auld Enemy'. It would be his last.

During his war with the Douglases he had become enchanted with the new technology – cannon. Mons Meg, the monster 'bombard' that sits on Edinburgh's walls to this day, was a gift from the Duke of Burgundy, his wife's uncle. He imported some state-of-the-art equipment from Flanders.

BY THE WAY: Even though the barrel was damaged in a ceremonial firing, Mons Meg was taken to the Tower of London after Culloden. Sir Walter Scott campaigned to have it brought back.

James II had made a couple of attacks on Berwick to no great effect (and an assault on the Isle of Man). Roxburgh was still in English hands, which was a sore point. James turned up and brought his new toys with him.

He took a hands-on approach to the technology and was standing close by when a cannon called 'the Lion' was fired. It exploded and he 'unhappily was slane with ane gun … which broke in the firing'.

Part of the casing ripped into his thigh, virtually severing his leg, he was 'stricken to the ground and died hastily'. He was 29.

James III – the one who was stabbed by a priest

History repeats, and once again Scotland had a child-king; he was 9 when he was crowned. Once again, the king was imprisoned by his own regents, this time the Boyd family.

How did James III complete Scotland?

Perhaps James III's greatest contribution to Scotland happened when he was 17. It didn't happen on the battlefield, but at the negotiating table.

A marriage was arranged with Margaret of Denmark. Her father, Christian I, the King of Denmark, was also King of Sweden and Norway. There was the outstanding matter of the Hebrides; Alexander III had arranged the purchase of the islands from

James III.

Norway for a flat sum PLUS an annual fee – and Scotland was in arrears. As part of Margret's dowry, the arrangement was annulled. Further, Shetland and Orkney were handed over, temporarily, in lieu of cash. The account was never settled and the Northern Isles became part of Scotland.

So it was under James III that Scotland became complete. The Hebrides was now Scottish, free and clear of any claim by Norway, though the Lords of the Isles might beg to differ. Shetland and Orkney were now Scottish.

How did he fall out with family?
James III went on to familiar Stewart territory: falling out with his brothers; both Alexander, Duke of Albany and John, Earl of Mar.

John was arrested on a charge of witchcraft and imprisoned in Craigmillar Castle. The story is that he was taken to Edinburgh for the good of his health; bleeding was a familiar Medieval treatment for just about any ailment – John was placed in a bath and bled to death.

James IV.

Alexander was harder to get rid of, as he had headed south and palled up with Edward IV of England. In 1482 he came home with an English army. He was calling himself 'Alexander IV'.

James III tried to raise an army to head off his brother and the English, but at Lauder he was arrested by his own nobles. He was kept in Edinburgh while Alexander ruled Scotland as 'Lord Lieutenant'. James eventually managed to convince enough nobles to turn back to him and Alexander fled. He ended up dead in a duel at a tournament in Paris.

James, meantime, was adding to the familiar Stewart family discord by favouring his second son, James, over his first-born heir, also bizarrely called James. As if Stewart names weren't confusing enough.

James the elder son, although still a boy, became the figurehead of a rebellion against his own father. The rebellion led to the Battle of Sauchieburn, where the king met his end.

There is a story that suggests a suitably bizarre end for a Stewart. Perhaps wounded, he got away from the field and called for a priest. A mysterious stranger stepped forward to minister to the king, then drew a dagger and stabbed him to death. A severe penance, perhaps.

James IV – the one that's buried under a pub

While James III's brutal penance at the hands of the mysterious priest was brief, James IV's would last a lifetime. He bore the guilt of his father's death heavily, although he had only been 15 at the time. He made numerous pilgrimages to holy places to seek forgiveness. He wore an iron chain around his waist, below his royal garments for the rest of his life.

Despite his iron underwear, he set about being a 'Good King' in a European style. He organised lavish public events, including tournaments where he was a valiant competitor himself. He travelled around the kingdom to greet his people and promoted law and order to the extent that there was a major drop in the crime rate. He was very well educated and supported the arts: literature, painting, poetry and music.

He made substantial improvements to the dreary castles of Edinburgh, Stirling, Linlithgow and Falkland. In Edinburgh he created a walled-in hunting garden including Arthur's Seat, which is the public Queen's Park we know today. He built a splendid new palace in the grounds of Holyrood Abbey. Holyrood Palace is the official Royal Residence in Scotland to this day.

The chief reason for this extravagance was to impress his new wife. She was used to better than draughty Scottish castles. After all, she was the daughter of the King of England!

How was James's biggest achievement his wedding?

Like his father, James III, James IV's biggest contribution to the story of Scotland was not by battle but by marriage.

Henry Tudor, King Henry VII, had almost NO royal lineage. He had become king by defeating Richard III in battle: he was a usurper and was well aware of it. He hastily ensured that his offspring would not be tarred with the same brush by marrying Elizabeth of York, who WAS a proper royal. She was the daughter of Edward IV and hence a descendant of the Scottish monarchy back to Malcolm Canmore and beyond. Henry Tudor was keen to suck in as much royal blood as he could to bolster his dynastic credentials. One daughter, Mary, would be Queen of France (briefly).

No matter what he might have thought about his power or prestige, a King of Scots was undeniably well connected, historically. So on 8 August 1503, Margaret Tudor, daughter of Henry VII, sister of Henry VIII, married James IV of Scotland.

James III's marriage had obtained Orkney and Shetland for Scotland. James IV's marriage would get the Stewart dynasty the Throne of England!

Margaret was somewhat upset to discover that Stirling Castle was home to a host of James's illegitimate children; he had been something of a lady's man. James and Margaret did manage to get along well enough to have six children, though only one would survive childhood.

With Margaret had come the 'Treaty of Perpetual Peace': peace between England and Scotland forever. It was a grand plan.

James IV had, however, neglected to abandon the long-standing 'Auld Alliance' with France. He was now bound in alliance with

England AND France, which would all be fine unless England and France went to war with each other. What were the chances of that happening? With Henry VIII on the throne, pretty likely.

Henry VIII had never renounced his claims in France. He went to war with Louis XII over the province of Anjou.

How did James end the 'Perpetual Peace'?

James IV in Scotland had to choose a side; despite pleading from his English wife, he chose France.

The terms of the Auld Alliance stated that if England attacked France then Scotland was duty bound to attack England, to deliver an attack from the rear and draw troops off the Continent. If Henry was defeated, James might have some chance of getting Northumbria back. **If** Henry VIII was defeated!

James attacked and took a couple of minor border castles. There was a plundering raid into England by a large party of Borderers. Henry, who was busy in France, sent an army under the Earl of Surrey.

The Scottish and English armies met in the Battle of Flodden.

For once the Scots had the greater forces (although not by a huge margin). They had the best position on the high ground of the battlefield. It should have been a win, but it wasn't. Somehow Scotland tends to do best when it is the underdog. Outmanoeuvred on the day, the Scots lost heavily; many thousands were slaughtered.

The well-known song 'Flowers o' the Forest' (although the current version is from the eighteenth century), captures it:

> Dule and wae for the order sent our lads to the Border;
> The English, for ance, by guile wan the day:
> The Flowers of the Forest, that foucht aye the foremost,
> The prime o' our land are cauld in the clay.

How did the king's head end up in a London pub?

James IV died heroically on the battlefield, or did he? No one recalls seeing him killed. The official story is that an English knight, Lord Dacre, found his body on the field, 'The dead body of the King of Scottes was found among the other carcasses in the fielde.'

There were some reports of him being seen after the battle and a rumour that he had retired to a life of prayer and contemplation.

However he died, the bizarre thing is what happened next. If you thought Robert Bruce's multi-site burial was weird, think again.

The king's remains were sent to Berwick and then to London. The royal coat, which had identified him, was sent to Catherine of Aragon, who forwarded it to her husband, Henry VIII, in France with the suggestion that he should fly it as a banner.

The embalmed body, wrapped in lead, arrived in London but could not be buried. The Pope was having problems with the French, so when James sided with them he excommunicated him. No Christian ground could accept such an unsanctified corpse. It was sent to Sheen Monastery and largely forgotten. The monastery's official function ended with Henry's dissolution, but the buildings and the king's remains were still there. An English writer was shown around the policies, 'I have been shewed the same body (as was affirmed) so lapped in lead throwne into an old wast roome, amongst old timber, stone, lead, and other rubble.'

The story then goes that a bunch of workmen found the considerably dilapidated corpse and proceeded to pull off the head and play football with it – as you do when you find a dead king.

Someone lifted the well-battered object and took it home as a souvenir. It was then given to St Michael's Church in London. At some point a sexton was told to take the unpleasant thing out and bury it in the grounds.

The church is long gone. A pub stands on the site. The discovery of the body of Richard III's body in a car park in 2012 has had lots of press, so why not a Scots king's head under the floorboards of a pub? 'The King's Head' would be an apt name for the pub, but it's not called that. It's called 'The Red Herring'. Which might be a perfect title for this whole story!

In Scotland, rumours were rife that while the English took away a body, it was not necessarily the king's – so where did he go?

He might possibly be a skeleton found in a well at Hume Castle; the Humes were definitely at the battle. This body had an iron chain round its waist – James had worn one for most of his life. A claim has also been made for bones found in Roxburgh Castle and for a graveside near Kelso.

If bones were gathered from these various contenders, DNA technology might provide an answer – this would require identifying a living descendant of James IV for comparison. The current Queen of England would be a perfect candidate.

James V – the one who died of a broken heart

Stewart history repeats itself again; James IV's oldest surviving son was 17 months old, so we are back with various forces vying for the regency and control of the country.

How did a Tudor queen get control of Scotland?

Tudor women, Queens Mary and Elizabeth, would prove themselves forceful, if not always stable. James V's mother, Margaret Tudor, was of the same stock (she was Henry VIII's sister). She also had a habit of picking unsuitable lovers, a trait that would prove a problem for her granddaughter, too.

Margaret Tudor took the position of regent according to her late husband's will, but there was a clause that stated that she would lose the privilege if she remarried. And she did, to a Douglas. Archibald Douglas, 6th Earl of Angus, was regarded as a dimwit, even by the other Douglases.

James V.

James's uncle, John Stewart, 2nd Duke of Albany, took control
and Margaret returned to England for a while. She bored quickly of
her Douglas husband and sidled up to her brother-in-law, Albany
(the man who had replaced her as regent). There was even a rumour
that the two might marry so that if anything happened to young
James they could start afresh.

She got her power back when James was 12 years old. She was
aided not by Douglas but by Douglas's mortal enemy, James
Hamilton, 1st Earl of Arran. She proclaimed her son old enough to
be king in his own right and positioned herself as his chief advisor.

The falling out with her Douglas husband went almost to open
warfare. When he approached Edinburgh she had the castle's cannon
fire on him. Douglas managed to turn the tables, seizing the young
king and holding him prisoner for three years.

Margaret, meanwhile, finally got a divorce from Archibald Douglas
(six years before brother Henry divorced Catherine of Aragon). She
then married Henry Stewart, who was made 1st Lord of Methven.
The third husband turned out to be as much of a disappointment as the
second; she tried to divorce him too and was denied.

How did the king get two French ladies?

It was in 1528 that James V finally escaped from his captors and took
up his kingship, when he was 16. The first order of business was
dealing with the hated Douglas. The key figures fled.

James V had to perform the royal duty of finding a suitable wife.
His father had married an English princess, he chose a French one.
It would be a short and sad affair. James travelled to France and
renewed the Auld Alliance. Despite the King of France's opinion that
his daughter was too sick, James married her – Madelaine of Valois.
The prediction was too true, Madelaine arrived in Scotland in May
and was dead by July.

James cast about again and caught Maria de Guise. She was not a princess and she had been married before, but she was of sturdy stock and she would prove herself no shrinking violet.

How was the king a wandering minstrel?

James V loved music. There is lovely story that he would, from time to time throw off his kingly robes and wander the countryside disguised as a wandering minstrel – a Gaberlunzie Man. He would call himself the 'Gudeman of Ballingeich'. It was said that he was a fine musician but as a singer his voice was 'rawky and harske'. This mingling with ordinary folk led some to call him the 'King of the Commons'.

He is even said to have written the 'Ballad of the Gaberlunzieman' ...

> The pawkie auld carle came o'er the lea,
> Wi' mony gude e'ens and days to me,
> Saying, Gudewife, for your courtesie,
> Will you lodge a silly poor man?

James's adventures outside his castles were not all such jolly affairs.

How was the score on a hunting trip deer nil, Borderers twenty-four?

During his reign James did try to tidy up some of the unruly parts of his kingdom. The free-lancing reivers of the Borderlands stole blatantly from Scots and English alike.

He set off on a hunting trip, with an entourage suitable for his purpose, to Ettrick Forest (pretty much Selkirkshire today).

He issued an invitation to the border gentlemen to join him there. Here was an opportunity for reconciliation – if they were prepared to swear loyalty all would be forgiven.

Young Johnnie Armstrong of Gilnockie, son of the Armstrong chief, turned up attired in fine style. The king was said to be angered that Johnny Armstrong turned up better dressed than he was himself. Reconciliation was not on the cards. The Borderers were overpowered.

Armstrong was reported to have said …

I am but a fool to seek grace at a graceless face, but had I known you would have taken me this day, I would have lived in the Borders despite King Harry (Henry VIII) and you both.

The entire Armstrong party was hanged, some accounts give the number as twenty-four.

War with England at last

After James's mother died there was not much to keep the peace with England. Henry VIII exhorted him to join his Protestant revolution, but James refused to even meet with him. That was enough of an insult to start a war. After a quick Scottish success at the Battle of Haddon Hill they had a humiliating defeat at the Battle of Solway Moss. Once again the Scots had superior numbers and should have known the terrain better, but bad judgment and lack of communication lost the day.

James died shortly afterwards on his sickbed in Falkland Palace. It was said that he died of a 'broken heart' because of the defeat, but he had already been ill and hadn't been at the battle. His only surviving child was a girl, Mary. She was now Queen of Scots!

STEWART TO STUART

JOHN KNOX – HE HAD FOUR MARYS

As we sit in the early sixteenth century the world is about to change. For the next few centuries conflict is about to be centred NOT on territory and wealth (although those never go away), it's going to be all about religion.

Throughout the previous centuries the Roman Catholic church had its own complicated history; nonetheless it had managed to become an overarching force. Monarchs across Europe could be turned around by threat of ex-communication, divine intervention and, basically, hell!

Officially the big challenge to this was in the 1530s when King Henry VIII of England resigned from the Roman Church and set up his own. This was a political (and partly economic) rather than religious dispute. For his subjects there were huge structural changes as Henry set about stripping the church establishment of both power and wealth, closing the monasteries, but there was not much change to the form of worship.

A more potent undercurrent was already under way. If you want a symbolic start date for this Protestant fundamentalism you could choose 31 October 1517, when Martin Luther nailed a document to a church door in Germany. The rest of the century would witness the often horrendous birth pangs of the new religion across Northern Europe. Scotland was no exception. It is often easier to get a grasp of a series of events when we have a central character (be they hero or villain) to pin the story to. In this case we have an outstanding candidate, John Knox.

John Knox

John Knox is remembered as a firebrand preacher, a religious zealot and a misogynist. To achieve what he did he must have had considerable charisma and he certainly had a reputation as an impressive performer in the pulpit. He was certainly unshakeable in his convictions. But a woman hater? Let's examine that accusation?

His anti-feminist reputation stems from a paper he wrote, *The First Blast of the Trumpet against the Monstrous Regiment of Women*. It haunted him for the rest of his life and his legacy ever since. He did not imagine a platoon of hideous females; his meaning of 'Monstrous' was 'unacceptable in the eyes of the Lord' and by 'regiment of Women' he meant the 'rule' of women. He was against female monarchs, which was a fairly common point of view at the time.

He did have a problem with women – SOME women. They were all called Mary.

Knox grew up in Haddington, raised by relatives. They were certainly not gentry, but they were not peasants either. John's brother got a start in trade, John got an education.

Knox and Marys.

d in France, but they did not set foot on the shore
be released. They were to be 'galley slaves'. The
ons of antiquity, Roman or Greek. As miserable
as in the Mediterranean, this was the North Sea!

ship that Knox met his second Mary – the
er of Christ. She did not appear in person but
cture was presented to the prisoners so that they
r. One of the men was so enraged by the blatant
was so much a part of the Roman church, that
and flung it over the side crying, 'Let our Lady
e is light enough: let her learn to swim.' It may
self.

g months, Knox was released and in England. He
each in the Church of England, although he had
s with the worship. It was not Protestant enough.
se firmly in charge as regent, Scotland was too
lly and literally given the awaiting stake). He
ld by preaching in the raucous border town of
d and moving to a ministry in Newcastle. In
o significant figures in his life and one of them

As a literate young man with no prospect of an inheritance, the obvious career path was the priesthood. That's what he did, he became a Roman Catholic priest (there weren't any other options). He did not advance immediately in the church but became a teacher.

His ears were open to some of the news from the Continent and the radical ideas it carried. He became friends with another young man, George Wishart, who had travelled to England and there had been convinced by the teaching of French thinker, Jean Calvin. John Knox was listening.

As he followed a small band accompanying George Wishart as he tried to spread his discoveries, he would have become painfully aware of his first Mary.

Who was the first Mary?

Maria de Guise or Lorraine, Mary of Guise, was already a widow at 19 when she came to Scotland. For all that she was Queen of Scots for a few brief years, she was always French and Catholic. If you want a face to put to the persecution and burning of early Protestants, it belongs to this elegant lady.

Mary de Guise.

As wife to James V she did her duty promptly, producing a son and heir and then a second boy, a spare, but tragedy struck. Both died on the same day; one was less than a year old, the other was less than a week. The best she could manage in the time left before her husband James died in despair after the Battle of Solway Moss was the birth of a girl.

Protecting that lassie, her inheritance and their religion became her life's work and she tackled it with vigour.

Although the child, Mary, was Queen of Scots from a few days old, she could clearly not rule; that job was for a regent. Mary of Guise wanted the job and she did get it, eventually. In the meantime she had to contend with James Hamilton, the 2nd Earl of Arran, in the post. He had the reputation of a vacillator. It was said that if he was for you before dinner he could be against you after. Mary took full advantage. Calling on her French connections, she had Hamilton awarded the title of Duke of Chatellerault and lands in France, hence Chatelerault park in Lanarkshire (the spelling was changed). It was not a smooth relationship, but she made it work for herself and her daughter.

England in the, not insubstantial, shape of Henry VIII, had an eye on Scotland and James V's death could be an opportunity. There was even a rumour that he might have taken Mary of Guise as his sixth wife, but the wee lassie was the main game. Hamilton supported the plan that the baby queen should be married to Henry's son, Edward. If they could be married at the youngest age possible Henry's Tudor dynasty would be Kings of Scotland. Problem solved.

Hamilton then reneged on the deal, no doubt influenced by Mary of Guise. Henry was not happy and sent substantial forces north to punish the Scots. The blow included a savage defeat for the Scots at the Battle of Pinkie at Musselburgh. The campaigns were known as 'the Rough Wooing'.

For 'safety' the baby queen was whisked off to France, where she was engaged instead to the Dauphin, heir to the throne of France. Her mum had done well.

With the lassie safely away, Mary of Guise could focus on dealing with these heretical Protestants.

How was John Kr
Meanwhile, Geor
vulnerable. John K
his mentor.

Mary's creature
cardinal's men bi
Knox and friend
Knox not to stru

There are man
in the sixteenth
jour; George Wi
fire was lit below
Some comments
this gunpowder
The last thing ye

There was
of gentlemen
St Andrews Ca
barricaded roo
cut it. They ra

With Ma
castle's defenc
St Andrews' I
porous block
among many

Letters w
was writing,
for the besi
were not En
at least Fife'

There w
were disen
castle wou
was reache
loaded ab
cause less

Galley slave
The prisoners arriv
– they were not to
phrase conjures vis
as that life was, it w

It was on boar
Virgin Mary, Mot
as a portrait. The pi
could pray before he
iconography, which
he seized the image
now save herself: sh
have been Knox him

After nineteen lor
obtained licence to p
fundamental problem

With Mary of Gu
hot for him (potenti
got as close as he cou
Berwick-upon-Twee
this period he met tw
was a woman.

John Knox.

How did John Knox have a lady friend?

Elizabeth Bowes came to him for spiritual guidance and she became his correspondent, confidante and, at times, companion for the rest of his life. There need not have been any impropriety, but the two did maintain a warm and close friendship for many years. Indeed, when the new church decided that celibacy for priests (which had been flagrantly flouted) was no longer required, the two decided that what Knox needed was a wife. She had to be suitably inclined, religious, preferably she should be literate and able to help John with his increasing burden of writing and correspondence. Where to find such a woman?

Elizabeth had one to hand – her daughter Marjorie. Elizabeth's husband, Marjorie's father, was utterly appalled by the suggestion, so it would be some years before the marriage actually took place.

How did Knox get involved in English politics?

The other person to enter his life was John Dudley, Duke of Northumberland. This was a dangerous man to be around. He took Knox under his wing and dragged him to the centre of English affairs.

Henry VIII died and was succeeded by his only son, Edward, a boy of 9 when he was crowned. He was a likeable, if rather intense, young man. He was intelligent and interested in all manner of things, including religion. He was de facto head of the Church of England, but he wanted to know more. He was fascinated by the new puritanical Protestants and invited some to discussions. Among these (thanks to the Duke of Northumberland) was wee John Knox frae Haddington.

Young Edward was shaping up to be a good king of England. But it was not be: in 1553, at the age of 16, the boy died. While he was ailing, Edward spent a great deal of effort on planning his own succession. Gloomy thoughts for an ill young lad. There was a scramble for the family tree and genealogical charts.

On paper the throne should go to Edward's half-sister, but she was the daughter of Catherine of Aragon, Henry VIII's first wife. She had never abandoned her divorced mother, nor her Catholic religion.

Another Mary was about to enter John Knox's life – Mary Tudor, soon to be Mary I of England – bloody Mary.

There had to be an alternative but the genealogical charts revealed nothing but girls. Mary Stewart was among them, but she was under the control of the French. The pin dropped on the 15-year-old Lady Jane Grey.

Very briefly, although it is a great story, Jane Grey had no more to worry about than finding a good country gentlemen and living a quiet life. Suddenly, with very little notice, she was declared Queen of England.

The population of England did not see this as acceptable. Mary was a known quantity, polite and fairly well liked. She was, after all, the actual daughter of good King Henry.

'Jane's army' was confronted by 'Mary's army' (with many defecting to Mary). Without too much hoo-ha, Mary won. The whole Lady Jane fiasco had been a scheme by Knox's mentor, the Duke of Northumberland.

Another Mary – the 'Bloody one'

Queen Mary started gently enough; it was some months before she cut the head off the teenaged Jane. Northumberland was similarly dealt with pretty promptly. She then turned to the business of God. This meant turning England back into a Catholic country, washing away the sins of her father. This was to be achieved by burning a few people – nearly 300 of them. As a radical Protestant preacher AND a protégé of Northumberland, John Knox's name was sure to be pretty high on that list. He left England.

He headed for Geneva to spend time with his spiritual guru, Jean Calvin. He was invited to lead the worship among Protestant refugees in Frankfurt; there was a brief visit to Scotland and then back to Geneva. This time he took with him his trusted Elizabeth and her daughter, Marjorie. Marjorie was, at last, his wife. They would have two sons together; these were happy times.

Trouble with the English

His greatest conflict was with Church of England exiles peddling their prayer book and other practices. It would be five years before he came home. His reputation as a preacher and a Protestant theologian grew. It was during this time that he wrote the *Monstrous Regiment of Women*.

By 1559 Bloody Mary had died and Elizabeth I was on the throne. England was Protestant again and many of the exiles could go home, but Knox had a problem. While the *Monstrous Regiment* was aimed at the Marys, Elizabeth read it as accusing her 'regiment' of being 'abhorrent in the eyes of God', simply because she was a woman. Knox's letters to her explaining that she had only to admit publicly that it WAS 'abhorrent' and she would get a dispensation from God, did not impress her much. She refused him entry to the country, even as a traveller en route to Scotland.

Hame
The Scotland that he returned to was both the same and very different. Mary of Guise was officially in charge as Regent of

Bloody Mary.

Scotland; however, the groundswell of support for Protestantism was an altogether stronger beast. Knox had not created it; he had been abroad, but his return was a spark that set the whole thing aflame. He preached in Perth and there was a riot, churches were attacked, icons were torn down. He preached in St Andrews and there was a riot, churches were attacked, icons were torn down (St Andrews Cathedral never recovered) … and then he headed for Edinburgh.

Meantime, Mary of Guise's army (mostly French) were on their heels, but there was no 'Protestant army' to engage in decisive battle, just unruly people. She called to France for help and the French arrived. For the second time under Mary's command, the French invaded Scotland (well, not Scotland, the Port of Leith).

At the request of the Scottish Protestants, an English army invaded and trapped the French in Leith. Two foreign armies were on Scottish soil. The stalemate held until June 1560, when Mary of Guise died. Under the 'Treaty of Edinburgh' the French went home, the English went home and Scotland's Protestant reformation became real.

On 1 August 1560 the Scottish Parliament renounced the jurisdiction of the Pope, abolished any objections to the reformed faith and banned the celebration of mass. Committees were appointed to work out how this new world order would work and John Knox was on all of them: he was writing the future of religion in Scotland.

He had been the defender of George Wishart. He had been a prisoner of the French. He was a personal friend of Calvin. He had been on the hit list of both Bloody Mary and Mary of Guise. He had been the warrior against the Church of England in Europe. Who better?

But that monumental year was not a year of euphoria for Knox; his wife Marjorie died.

Final decisions on some proposals were held pending, waiting for the arrival in Scotland of the Queen of Scots!

MARY THE LASSIE

Stewart or Stuart?

The question is often asked – which is correct SteWEart or StUart? The answer is, both are right and both are wronging depending on when you are talking about. At the age of 5, Mary SteWEart went to France. When she came back at the age of 19 she was Mary StUart. The revised spelling was for the benefit of the French, who had no letter W in their alphabet. Her son, James, and all the following Stewarts were now Stuarts with a U. This did not apply to all the other Stewarts (related or otherwise) living in Scotland.

Mary the Lassie

Asking various audiences which Kings of Scots they have heard of, the only woman who ever gets a mention is Mary, Queen of Scots. Her story has been told in biographies, dramas and movies. She gets a lot of attention. That said, a recent survey of the Scottish public

Young Mary.

revealed that more than half didn't recognise her portrait. According to the survey, the best-known facts about her were that she had red hair and was accused of killing her husband. Fewer than one in five knew she was Queen of Scots while a baby.

In the long line of Stewart child monarchs Mary wins the prize – she was queen from 6 days old.

Please remember when you consider her actions during her time in Scotland, she was only a lassie. She was 18 when she got here, she was 24 when she left. If you think she was unwise in some of her decisions, think about her situation.

Queen of Scots from six days, Queen of France at 15 and first in line to be Queen of England – she was a red-hot royal property.

Growing up in the French Royal court from the age of 5, she was good looking, charming and intelligent, an accomplished musician and a sportswoman. She was multi-lingual (including Scots). She had high status as the fiancée of the heir to the French crown and everybody loved her (except her future mother-in-law, Catherine de Medici). It must have been an idyllic childhood – but it was all to go wrong.

She married the young Francis at 14 (he was a year younger) and was crowned queen the following year, but it was not to last. After just a year and a half Francis died after an ear infection turned septic. Mary was heartbroken. For all that their marriage had been arranged, there was every indication that the two genuinely liked each other.

Catherine de Medici leapt into the promotion and protection of her younger son, Charles, and quickly made it clear there was no place for young Mary.

HOMECOMING

She had little alternative but to head homeward. She arrived at the Port of Leith on 19 August 1561. It was not the best time for a Catholic lassie with a French accent to come to Scotland.

Her mother, Mary of Guise, who had campaigned so vigorously for her religion and Mary's interests, had just died. The

Scottish Parliament was in the hands of the Protestants, who had just effectively banned Roman Catholicism. John Knox was in St Giles' Cathedral.

Who could she turn to? There were still a good number of Catholic nobles, but if they were expecting Mary to charge in as a firebrand leading a Catholic rebellion, they were to be disappointed. On the one hand she sought peace and reconciliation with the Protestants, on the other she absolutely refused to abandon her own personal faith.

A quick conversion to Protestantism would have helped in Scotland. The memory of Mary de Guise was very fresh and the Protestants had just won. A young Stewart queen might have been just the thing to pull the country together – if only she would toe the line.

A quick conversion to Protestantism would also have helped with her claim to her (potential) third crown – England! She had, as events would prove after her death, the foremost claim of anyone in the world to be a Tudor heir since her granny was Henry VIII's sister. Meantime, Elizabeth was on the throne. The only person that could better Mary's claim was any offspring of Elizabeth, but Elizabeth was, famously, the Virgin Queen.

A Protestant Mary would have had a good deal of support as Elizabeth's heir, but Mary had another problem. In England she had support from a group of supporters who would ultimately lead to her death.

There was a body of thought that Elizabeth was NOT a rightful queen. If Catherine of Aragon was NOT divorced from Henry (and the Pope said she wasn't), then Elizabeth was a bastard and should not reign. This group asserted that Elizabeth should immediately be stripped of her crown and the next legitimate heir be installed. That would be Mary Stewart, Queen of Scots. These people were English Catholics and they loved Catholic Mary!

Being Protestant would have been good for Mary's health, but, on a personal level, she would not budge. She had masses said (privately) in Holyrood Palace – this was technically illegal. This iniquity was condemned from the pulpit of St Giles by John Knox. She was his Fourth Mary!

Who was on her side?

It must have been a huge shock to the lassie, still only 18, to come from the luxury of the French court to dreich Scotland, dour surroundings and an even dourer reception. A potential ally was James Stewart, her half-brother: the Earl of Moray. He was the son of James V and, by all accounts, a very competent young man. Mary's problems were that there were many who thought James would make a much better monarch than the 'French lassie' and that he was very Protestant. James's problem was that he was illegitimate.

For a while she kept her brother on-side (she was his wee sister) and for a while managed to keep out of political wrangling. Instead, she attempted to reconstruct, as best she could, the pleasures of the French court. Historian Magnus Magnusson paints the picture; 'It was crowded with scholars, poets, artists, and musicians. There were much dancing and merry-making, much playing of billiards, cards, and dice late into the night, and much riding and hunting during the day.'

How would a husband help?

Mary's problems were then escalated by another Stewart – Henry, Lord Darnley. She had the Scottish crown and, potentially, the crown of England and she had French connections (not to mention being witty, attractive and intelligent). Mary was the most eligible widow in Europe.

Yet she married Darnley. He had credentials; he had the same granny, Margaret Tudor, which made him a potential candidate for the English crown. He was also a genuine royal Stewart, his line going back to James II, and he was Catholic.

There has been a trend in recent years for historians to revisit persons that have been blackened in history, to try to find the better side of them (Queen Anne and even Mary I are examples), but there are not many apologists for Lord Darnley. Magnus Magnusson described him as 'shallow, vain, weak, indolent, selfish, arrogant, vindictive and irremediably spoiled'. Historian James Froude said he was, 'like a child who has drifted from the shore on a tiny pleasure boat, his sails, puffed out with vanity'. Darnley quickly revealed that he saw marriage as no impediment to his previous pastimes of heavy drinking and womanising.

Darnley.

He was a disappointment to Mary from the outset and he was less than happy with her. Given his ancestry he had assumed that he would be appointed joint monarch, King of Scots. Given the general tendency towards the assumption of male dominance, he fancied that he would soon rule the country. Mary's answer was a vehement 'NO!'

Meantime, the marriage had lost her the support of her half-brother, Moray. He allied with other Protestant lords and raised a force. In response, an official 'Queen's' army was raised. For a few months the two armies rattled around Scotland without seriously coming to blows: it is known as the Chaseabout Raid.

Mary's military hand was strengthened by the arrival (from exile in France) of another dubious character, Bothwell. To give him his name, rank and number he was James Hepburn, 4th Earl of Bothwell. He stepped in to support her. She may have viewed him as sort of saviour, but he was no knight in shining armour.

Who was her pal, Rizzio?
The next episode is one of the best-known stories in Scottish history. Mary was trying to keep her cultural passions alive; embroidery,

intelligent conversation, music. Her husband had no part in this cosy world – she was trying to avoid him as far as possible. One of her key companions was an Italian musician, David Rizzio. He was good company, a friend and a confidante perhaps – but the excluded Darnley did not see it like that.

He joined a gang of men who stormed into Mary's chamber and dragged out the gentle Rizzio. He was stabbed over fifty times; a dramatic scene, which has been reproduced in several paintings (and movies). The best place to hear the story is in Holyrood House in the room where it occurred. There are even a few blotches on the stairs that may be Rizzio's blood! There is nothing better than a bit of gore (however faint) to enliven a good tale.

Mary was already pregnant with Darnley's child. On 19 June 1566 James Stuart was born.

Darnley was by now loathed by people from all views and persuasions. It should have been no great surprise that he found himself dead, though the exact details are still a matter of debate. He had fallen ill and Mary had invited him back from Glasgow to recover, installing him in a house at Kirk o' Fields. Mary had the good grace to visit him.

Rizzio murder.

On a February night the house was rocked by a large explosion. Darnley was found lying in a neighbouring garden, but he was not ripped apart by the blast nor burned by the ensuing fire: there wasn't a mark on him. It is likely that he had been smothered – the exact sequence of events is not known.

Why not try another bloke?

Who could have carried out such a deed? A lot of fingers were pointing at the Earl of Bothwell. He was tried for the murder, but the trial was rushed through before Darnley's family could gather their evidence and he was acquitted. Now he was ready to show his hand.

In a pub in the Cannongate he persuaded gentlemen including eight bishops, nine earls and seven lords to sign a paper supporting his plan: he was going to marry the queen.

Days afterward he met Mary on the road back from Stirling, where she had just seen her 10-month-old son for the last time. He escorted Mary to Dunbar castle.

Mary claimed that she had no willing hand in any of this. She may have been totally unaware of the bond signed by the bishops and earls. She claimed that, rather than a romantic interlude in Dunbar, she had been abducted and raped by Bothwell.

Whatever the truth, matters were out of Mary's hands. Bothwell had openly declared he would marry the queen. He had (almost certainly) removed her husband, by murder. He had another small detail to contend with – he was already married. On 3 May he managed to get a divorce and on the 15th he married Mary, Queen of Scots.

Just about everyone was outraged. Bothwell tried to organise an army. They met Mary's half-brother Moray's army at Carberry Hill but there was no battle and Bothwell walked away. Mary was taken, as a prisoner, to Edinburgh and then to an island in Loch Leven; there she was forced to sign away her crown.

ESCAPE TO PRISON

After the best part of a year she escaped, aided by the Douglases. An army was raised and quickly defeated by Moray. In a small fishing boat, she left Scotland for the last time. It was a sad end to the reign of Mary; she had been in Scotland for less than seven years – it had been a rough ride. She was still only 25.

Moray, after some further skirmishes, took charge of Scotland and the baby James.

Mary was starting what would be nineteen years as a prisoner in England. She might have expected support from her cousin Elizabeth, but she was a woman under suspicion. Was Mary guilty or innocent?

In the first place the charges were adultery and murder. Had she had illicit relations with Rizzio or Bothwell? Had she been complicit in the murder of Darnley?

There is no real evidence to convict her, except for a casket of incriminating documents, which may well have been forgeries.

In England the question would become was she guilty or innocent of conspiring against Queen Elizabeth.

To many Catholic English gentlemen, Mary was the perfect figurehead to lead a revolt to oust Elizabeth and overturn Protestant England. They had only to come up with the perfect plan. There were several attempts, including the Ridolfi Plot, the Throckmorton Plot and the Babington Plot. In each case there was the suggestion that Mary was involved at some level. In each case that amounted to suspicion of treason and that suspicion led directly to her execution – thanks to the machinations of the Catholic gentlemen.

And was she guilty? There is precious little evidence.

KNOX AGAIN

So what part did John Knox play in Mary's downfall? Not a lot, apart from a general resentment of her gender and religion. Unlike her mother, Mary of Guise and the English Bloody Mary, Mary the Lassie was never a threat to Knox.

The day after her arrival in Scotland she had proclaimed that she was not challenging the religious status quo but herself and her servants should be left in peace. The following Sunday Knox made clear from the pulpit that any illegal Popish activities should not be tolerated. It was clearly directed against Mary.

Mary challenged him to debate face to face. She was a brave lassie since, as much as Knox was renowned as a fiery preacher, he was equally known as a ferocious debater.

Mary pointed out that he had incited rebellion against her mother and 'The Monstrous Regiment' issue naturally came up; it was a direct challenge to Mary's own situation. Knox did concede that he was willing to accept her rule 'as long as her subjects found it convenient'. He did also assert that should any monarch exceed their limits they should be opposed, even by violence. That much had been enshrined for the Scots in the Declaration of Arbroath 240 years before.

They met, at Mary's request, several times and each time Mary came away frustrated and angry. On one occasion she burst into tears. Knox tried to console her, 'Madam …, I never delighted in the weeping of any of God's creatures; … much less can I rejoice in Your Majesty's weeping.'

Of course, when the whole Rizzio/Darnley/Bothwell drama enfolded, Knox joined in the general condemnation of her as adulteress and murderer and called for her execution, but over the course of their relationship what did John Knox do to Mary, Queen of Scots?

He made the lassie cry!

How did Knox get on with other women?

As for Knox's personal relationships with women? He lost his good wife, Marjorie, around 1560, leaving him with two sons. He still had the companionship of her mother, Elizabeth Bowes, his long-time friend and confidante.

Four years after Marjorie's death he married again, to Margaret Stewart, which raised a few eyebrows. She was 17, daughter of a

Scottish nobleman, while he was 54. She took on Marjorie's role as secretary and became his nurse when his health failed. It was not just a marriage of convenience – they had three daughters.

So did John Knox have a problem with women? Beyond the universal sexism of the time, perhaps not. He did have a problem with Marys.

THE WISEST FOOL

James VI was yet another in the line of child monarchs: he was crowned at the ripe old age of 13 months. He had already lost his mother, who had been imprisoned in Loch Leven and escaped from there to England, never to come to Scotland again.

The official regent was his (illegitimate) uncle, James Stewart, Earl of Moray. The boy-king suffered a fearsome Presbyterian education at the hands of several tutors. He grew up intelligent, quick-witted and highly literate.

How did James start burning witches?

Incidents surrounding his marriage inflamed a dark side of James's soul. A match was arranged with Anne, Princess of Denmark, and she was to sail across to Scotland but the ship was beaten back by North Sea storms. James went to fetch her himself. While in Denmark, he continued to further his education by consulting with experts in various subjects. He came back much better informed on the subject of witchcraft.

On the return journey the king's ship ran into bad weather and nearly came to grief in the Firth of Forth. James needed something to blame; he chose witchcraft.

A raft of suspects were rounded up and the story was eventually confessed (much of it under torture). It went like this ...

A coven of witches had a regular get-together in St Andrews' kirk in North Berwick – they decided to drown the king. A black cat was obtained and christened 'James'. The cat, tied up with bones scavenged from a graveyard, was passed backwards and forwards over a fire with suitable incantations. The witches then set sail on the Firth in sieves (it had to be a 'mission impossible' to prove it could only have been achieved by witchcraft). The cat was then cast into the sea, creating a storm to sink the king.

This was the chain of events accepted by the court in the 'North Berwick Witch Trials'. Up to seventy were arrested. These included; the 4th Earl of Bothwell (nephew to Queen Mary's Bothwell), he escaped from Edinburgh Castle; John Fian, a local schoolteacher who was marked as ringleader; Barbara Napier, a lady of good standing. Many of the others such as Gillies Duncan and Agnes Sampson were simple countrywomen.

The guilty were executed by fire. It is not clear how many met that fate.

James VI took a personal interest in the trial and would go on to write the learned volume *Daemonologie* on the subject of witchcraft. Persecution of witches was widespread across Europe, but the Scots indulged with particular enthusiasm. It is reckoned that 3,000 to 4,000 men and women were executed.

KING OF ENGLAND

Mary, Queen of Scots had been a danger to Elizabeth I precisely because Mary did have a perfectly righteous claim to the English throne. Her son had the same. When the 'Virgin Queen' died, James was next in line.

He set off from Edinburgh with a considerable entourage, leaving behind a promise to visit home every year. He made his way through England, inviting himself to stay at various grand houses along the way.

He arrived in London and was crowned James I, King of England, on 25 July 1603. The English hadn't a clue what to make of him!

How did the English like James?
His personal hygiene left something to be desired. He had no care for the finer points of court etiquette, he loved fart jokes and bawdy tales. He would soon show that he preferred the company of good-looking young men to any of the Ladies of Court and would openly show his affection to his boys. He was bold and forthright with

everyone, not least those of high rank, noble or churchman. And he spoke in that grating Scotch tongue!

> His sense of humour matches his personal habits; always coarse and anatomical, it rose sometimes to 'a fluorescence of obscenity'.
>
> J.P. Kenyon

On the other hand, they were surprised to find that he was intelligent and organised. He had no problem coming to a decision, which was a relief after the constant dithering of his predecessor. He would listen to people and, above all, he understood politics.

He had grown up trying to hold the vying factions together in Scotland and now applied that experience with a keen mind in England. He had many factions to deal with here and he played a canny game.

Catholic conspirators had been the bane of his mother's life and they had not gone away. The Gunpowder Plot of 1605 could have been catastrophic. If the bomb had gone off (and it would have been a big bang) on the occasion of the opening of Parliament it would have taken out the king AND the Privy Council AND the entire Parliament. The entire governmental structure of England was in that building and everybody was there on that day. It could have led to anarchy.

James VI, London.

> BY THE WAY: There is a suspicion now that government officials knew about the plot from an early stage but held off from intervening so they could catch them in the act, to make sure it was big news.

Unlike some of his predecessors, James did not immediately set about purging Catholics. He would rather keep them on side; they owed him one.

How did James make the Bible?

He had another religious problem – the Protestants, or rather two conflicting types of Protestants. There was the Church of England of which he was official head, and the growing ranks of Puritans, who must have reminded him of the Presbyterians back home.

He challenged them both to work on a new landmark project. One that would create a legacy that any monarch would be proud of: the King James Bible.

He invited the Church of England representatives to discuss the project, who arrived thinking they had won the commission. He sat them down (on uncomfortable benches) and barraged them with complex theological questions and erudite arguments, for hours.

He did exactly the same with the Puritans.

He ended up with six committees. Documents written by committee are not always the most coherent, but this one worked.

Some seriously good academic explorations of the Hebrew, Greek and Aramaic texts went on, and both sides made concessions. The result was the most successful printed book ever issued.

There were different Bibles before and there have been different Bibles since – James's has stood the test of time.

It strikes the authors that the dominant literary form of the time was drama (and poetry); it was the era of Shakespeare. The King James Bible fits that context. It works well read aloud; it was designed to be performed.

PLANTATION

James was a champion of the idea of 'Plantation'. Instead of vanquishing a region and maintaining it with an (expensive) garrison, you flood it with people who are, at least nominally, friendly to you. He tried the theory out across the Atlantic in Virginia, based at JAMEStown, and in Bermuda.

Closer to home, he planted the north of Ireland, with consequences to this day.

Queen Elizabeth had spent decades (and a fortune) trying to solve the 'Irish Problem'. There had been attempts to colonise it before but they had failed because local opposition was too strong. James inherited a different situation. The wildest, most untameable and most Irish part of the island, the north, had just been through the Nine Years' War. England had won. The Irish leader, Hugh O'Neill, surrendered to a portrait of the queen, unaware that she was already dead.

O'Neill and several of the leading chieftains had left in 'The Flight of the Earls'. The country was defeated and leaderless. For James there couldn't have been a better time.

James's plantation led to the strong Protestant Ulster presence that celebrates Ulster–Scots culture enthusiastically. The Plantation wasn't all Scottish; 40 per cent of the settlers were from England.

> BY THE WAY: If you suggest to some Ulster Protestants that their ancestors might have been English they get very upset.

There were four separate plantation schemes; the settlement of O'Cahan Country (now County Londonderry) was by the London Guilds and was entirely English. James's main Official Plantation, which covered most of the province, was settled by both Scottish lowlanders and English. There were two that were both entirely Scottish; North Antrim and North Down. Both are interesting stories.

BY THE WAY: When Ulster Presbyterians rose in revolt
against the British government in the 'United Irishman's
Rising' of 1789, North Antrim and North Down were the two
areas that rose.

James also commissioned the Plantation of the Isle of Lewis by
'Gentlemen Adventurers of Fife' in order to subdue the unruly
islanders. It did not go well.

THE MIDDLE SHIRES

The Borderlands were an embarrassment. How could James run a
co-ordinated kingdom when any gentleman or trader (Scots or Irish)
travelling north–south had to run the gauntlet of bands of fearsome
outlaws – the border reivers. Farmers on either side of the line had
every chance of finding their stock gone in the morning.

He tried to do away with the troubles by declaring the region the
'Middle Shires'. He came down heavily on the fiercely independent
border reiver families. Reivers, or anyone associated with them,
were subject to summary justice – with on-the-spot executions.
Strongholds were burned and many of the remaining people were
'cleared'. Many found themselves in Ulster, where border names are
still common.

To achieve his aim he recruited two local men, Walter Scott and
Robert Kerr, both notorious reivers. Both turned coat on their
neighbours and former allies and did the dirty work. As reward they
became the Earl of Buccleuch and the Earl of Roxburgh respectively,
and both accumulated huge amounts of land in the process.

JUDGING JAMES

'Jamie Saxt', James VI & I, is a hard man to pin down. It is appropriate that the best-known quote about him is an inherent contradiction – 'the wisest fool in Christendom' (attributed to the King of France).

He was certainly a peacemaker. The constant round of war with France or Spain or Netherlands paused throughout his reign. Wars cost money; he didn't like spending money.

James had united the crowns. He would dearly have liked to have made a greater union. He tried to unite the churches by sending his Church of England north, but he had the savvy not to push his luck on that one (unlike his son).

BY THE WAY: When you look at the British flag – the Union Jack: a conjunction of the cross of St George, the Saltire of St Andrew and the Red Saltire of St Patrick, remember that it was commissioned by a Jacobite – James VI and I.

He did promote the notion of the 'Divine Right of Kings', which is an ancient concept. James embraced it, he even wrote a book about it, the *Basilikon Doron* (royal gift) – in defiance of the Declaration of Arbroath, which maintained that kings could be replaced if it was the will of the people, 'The state of monarchy is the supremest thing upon earth, for kings … even by God himself, they are called gods.'

While he may have believed that he was 'Gods' Lieutenant' on earth, he also understood that he had to accommodate the earthly powers around him; people, nobles and churches.

'Divine Right' would turn out to be a sour gift for his son.

THE STUART
WARS

'Ye Jacobites by name'
With only the most fleeting glimpse of Scottish history, the term
Jacobite will quickly crop up. Less common is an understanding of
what it means. If the term was 'Jamesite' it might be more obvious.
Jacobi is the Latin for James, hence Jacobite. Broadly, it means
supporter of the Stewart/Stuart dynasty, which makes sense since,
with a spectacular lack of imagination for Christian names, all of the
Stewart kings, apart from a couple of early Roberts and a couple of
late Charlies, were called James; eight of them.

Jamesite or Jacobite could apply to royal supporters from the birth
of James I in 1406 to the death of James VIII in 1766 (360 years), but it
has generally been associated with the period in which the Stuarts lost
the throne of England and went to some lengths to get it back. That is
James VII and VIII – two James bookended by a couple of Charlies.

What about the ladies?
A lot of the trouble in this period came down to the violent assertion
(by a powerful enough section of the population) that the English
monarch could not be a Catholic. But consider the consequence of
another block to the royal seat – sex. England had fairly recently had
a Queen Mary and a Queen Elizabeth, and then there was a Queen
Mary II and an Queen Anne. Under 'special circumstances' queens
and even queens regnant (ruling queens) were not an alien concept.
Yet if females had been counted in their own right, rather than as a
last resort, the royal line (and history) might have been very different.

On the death of James VI (or I) his oldest-surviving offspring
was Elizabeth. If she had become Elizabeth II, England would never

have had the prickly Charles I. Without his notorious self-belief and intransigence there might have been no War of the Three Kingdoms, no English Civil War and no ensuing problems with James VII. Elizabeth did have her place in creating dynasties as her grandson was, controversially, to become George I. Mind you, had she been heiress to the throne it was unlikely she would have married such a nobody as Frederick V of Bohemia!

Again, when Charles II died without a legitimate heir, his sister Mary was next oldest. She could have sidelined James VII and all the bother that he caused. She did eventually become Mary II, alongside her husband (and first cousin) William III. Then again, how would he have ranked among the suitors that would have swarmed around a latent monarch?

Just saying.

Which war?
If we discount all the Stewart tribulations before the Union of the Crowns, and agree that the Jacobite cause was principally (though certainly not entirely) about placing a Stuart back on the English throne, then the shenanigans in the eighteenth century (including the '15 and the '45) was only the final instalment in a long story. In terms of this definition you could easily say that the story started in 1649, almost a hundred years before Culloden. There was a considerable amount of upheaval before and following this date that break down into three separate wars.

They all boil down to the support for a Stuart King. '**The 'Stuart Wars'**.

THE WAR OF THE THREE KINGDOMS

The War of the Three Kingdoms is EPIC! It is exhilarating and utterly horrifying. It has battles that swing from certain victory to abject defeat. It has military miracles and farcical failings. It has characters and whole kingdoms switching sides. It has heroes and villains in plenty; the intransigent Charles, the flamboyant Prince Rupert, the complex Cromwell.

It is also set in an age that, with the development of cheap printing and an increased reading public, pretty much saw the birth of journalism. Much was written and published at the time, most of it unashamedly supporting one faction or another. It was an age where propaganda became a weapon of war.

The War of the Three Kingdoms resulted, directly and indirectly, in something of the order of 200,000 deaths. It was, above all, complicated. There have been attempts to explain through drama, documentary and drama documentary. It would take something on the scale of the seventy-three episodes of *Game of Thrones* to even come close.

Even restricting things to the Scottish perspective, a few pages in this book can only give a quick sketch. Scotland has plenty of drama and its own lead characters – Leslie, Murray, MacColla. It is complicated. 1649 is often mentioned as a starting point for the wars to defend the Stuarts, but the kick-off was a few years before that. And it was the Scots that kicked the first ball!

Everyone has heard of the English Civil War (rounds one and two) in which Englishmen fought with fellow Englishmen, but that was only part of it. A more accurate description was 'The War of the Three Kingdoms'; England was only one of the three.

The English Civil War led to the overthrow and indeed the execution of a Stuart king by a section of the English population. The War of the Three Kingdoms involved Stuart attackers and defenders in Scotland and Ireland and sometimes England. This was followed by Cromwell's attempt to stamp out support for the Stuarts in England, Scotland and Ireland.

Through all the conflicts the Scottish position is complicated.

How was Charles 'divine?

Charles I had inherited the idea of 'Divine Right' from his father; he was, he had no doubt, appointed by God to rule – 'A little god on earth'. Like his father, he had no problem accepting that in England he was (thanks to Henry VIII) head of the church. Charles's difficulty was that he lacked his father's pragmatism; rather than working his way around problems he tended to attack them head on. His problem in England was money. His problem in Scotland was religion.

In England he had to suffer Parliament. He had the power to summon or dismiss it but he failed, to his chagrin, to control it – and, ultimately, he couldn't ignore it. Parliament, House of

Charles I.

Lords and House of Commons, was made up of the nobility and the land-owning gentry. In theory most of the national power was in the king's hands, but the Parliament did hold one valuable asset – the purse strings. These land owners each controlled the only effective administrative infrastructure within their own personal domains. Without their co-operation there was no effective way of gathering taxes.

The king did have a variety of ways of raising funds. Charles exploited these to the full and tried some creative ways of expanding them, but income was way short of expenditure. The shortfall required the intervention of Parliament. When additional, unexpected, bills came in Parliament had to be convinced and few things are more expensive than war! And war was on its way. With Scotland.

THE BISHOP WARS

How was Charles's church a problem?

Charles I's problem with Scotland was religion. It was not even a Protestant–Catholic collision (his son, James VII, would kick that particular ball back on to the pitch), it was between two varieties of protestants.

James VI had grown up with the Church of Scotland. The Scottish Parliament had abolished the jurisdiction of the Pope in Scotland five years before he was born. The church's shadow had hung heavy over his early years and his education; he had constantly to work to keep on their good side. In England he had Anglicans and Puritans to manage.

Charles I had grown up with the Church of England. This Anglican Church was founded on Henry VIII's need to shed the rule of the Pope in Rome, but there was no great doctrinal problem – many aspects of actual worship changed little.

The Protestant church in Scotland was a different beast entirely. It had been influenced by thinking from the Continent, principally German. It had grown from the grass roots, with a lot of struggle along the way. It was, in some ways, the polar opposite of a church founded by Royal Decree for royal convenience and many Scots regarded Anglicanism as little better than Popery without the Pope.

Charles was somewhat miffed that only one of his three

kingdoms recognised him as head of the church. In at least one kingdom, the place where he was born, he could do something about it. Couldn't he?

His father had envisioned a 'Union of Churches' to follow the 'Union of Crowns', but James was far too 'wise' to push the Scottish Church too hard. Charles was not so subtle.

There were many issues that divided the two churches, but it boiled down to two – bishops and books. The appetites and iniquities of the clergy, in particular bishops (who had been lavishly conspicuous in their consumption), had been a major complaint that led to 'Protest' in the first place. Both in Scotland and on the Continent.

The Calvinistic assertion was, very strongly, that the Holy Bible was the absolute Word of God and that NO other texts were necessary. Charles tried to impose a *Book of Canons* and then a new *Book of Common Prayer* in line with the English church; to the Scots this smacked of nothing short of Popery.

Jenny Wha Hae!

The next event lit the flame below a simmering of pot of discontentment that bubbled and boiled and led to fourteen years of bloodshed. Leading the charge was a wee thirty-something Edinburgh wifey in a bonnet. The weapon? A three-legged stool.

Of course, there are all sorts of people involved and all sorts of issues at stake, but history loves a heroine – a female warrior! Here we have the poster girl for Scottish Protestantism: Jenny Geddes.

When, in 1637, a service was held in St Giles' Cathedral, the High Kirk of Scotland (John Knox's own pulpit) to introduce the *Book of Common Prayer*, resentment was simmering. It was Jenny Geddes who picked up a three-legged stool and hurled it, yelling 'daur ye say mass in my lug!'

The rest of the congregation joined in, chucking whatever could be chucked, smashing windows and creating mayhem, before spilling out on to the streets, where it quickly developed into a full-on Edinburgh mob. Edinburgh folk have always been game for a good riot. The rioting spread, erupting in towns across Scotland. The Church and Parliament had to regain control. Their answer was the

The Great Montrose

In 1655 the pro-Stuart cause had a victor, a 'blood red comet crossing the shuddering midnight'. A truly swashbuckling Jacobite hero a full century before Bonnie Prince Charlie: Montrose. To give him his name, rank and number he was James Graham, 1st Marquis of Montrose. He has been described as Scotland's greatest ever military commander. George Gilfillan in Martyrs and Heroes of the Scottish Covenant refers to him as 'Scotland's Napoleon'.

> He left a name at which the world grew pale,
> To point a moral, or adorn a tale

Above his tomb is the inscription 'Ne Oublie', do not forget. But how many remember him?

Before we consider whether Montrose's military reputation was justified, let us introduce you to another character. A Highlander. A genuine 'Highland Rogue'. He was known as 'The Destroyer' or 'The Devastator'. He led his ragtag warriors in a 'Year of Victories', winning battle after battle, often against overwhelming odds. He used the Highland landscape as a weapon of war. He established the ferocious reputation of the Highland warrior. He invented the infamous 'Highland charge'. He firmly established the Highlands as a potentially powerful and dangerous military and political entity.

'Fear thollaidh nan tighean'

The name of this glorious Scottish hero was Alasdair MacColla Chiotach MacDhomhnaill. You've probably never heard of him. I make the point repeatedly that how a person appears in the nation's historical memory comes down to how their story was told. So why was Alasdair MacColla's story not told?

The point is that it was! Loudly and eloquently:

> Alasdair Mhic o ho
> Cholla Ghasda o ho
> As do laimh-s' gun o ho
> Earbainn tapaidh trom eile

Where he does appear in the propaganda press he is a monster. But his song was sung (and still is) throughout Highland culture. When he went on campaign he took with him not a painter, but a poet, Iain Lom MacDonald of Keppoch. His wit and verse skills were such powerful weapons in the Highlands that the Campbells put a price on his head.

In music and verse MacColla's story was told – in Gaelic. In the ancient tradition it was kept safe by bards and passed mouth to mouth, heart to heart. The lines above are sung today by the Scottish band Capercaillie and Irish band Clannad, among others. Always in Gaelic.

In keeping with the oral tradition, MacColla approaches mythical status. He is a giant (over 7ft tall) with a legendary sword (which was exhibited in Ireland for many years before disappearing). He had a miraculous birth, 'The night that Alasdair MacColla was born the swords leapt out of their scabbards, the shields clanged together on the wall and the mares cast their foals.' He was 'fear thollaidh' – the Devastator, or Destroyer

Keep in mind, when considering the Highlanders' role in the campaign of Bonnie Prince Charlie a century later, that those men would have been entirely aware of the stories of Alasdair MacColla and his Year of Victories.

There is another point to be borne in mind when wondering about his place in Scotland's story. Who exactly was he fighting against? Who exactly where these victories over? Well, the Scots! More specifically the Scottish Parliament. Some call this the Scottish Civil War.

And on whose behalf, exactly, was he fighting? That we'll have to see.

The Ulster Rebel?
Alasdair MacColla was a MacDonald. A son of Coll, from the island of Colonsay in the Hebrides. When he enters this story he is staying with kinsmen the MacDonnells in Ulster. The 1641 rebellion against the Ulster Plantation broke out. Alasdair's host, Randal Og MacDonnell, the Earl of Antrim, was heavily invested in the plantation. His father had successively manipulated events so that he was the only 'Gaelic' chieftain to retain significant territory in Ulster.

He had achieved this by conducting his own private plantation of Protestant Scots on part of his lands. He also seems to have had some sort of favour with James VI.

The rebellion was not in Randal's interests. He formed a militia against the rebels, enlisting the young MacColla. Alasdair's sympathies were not naturally with the authorities; he switched sides and served as a commander under Felim O'Neill. His reputation grew and he was responsible for devastating much of County Down. It was said that in his clearance of settlers in County Down, even cattle and sheep were slaughtered for being English.

Alasdair and his relative, Randal MacDonnell, did end up on the same side. More or less. As events in England unfolded, Randall proved himself to be a committed Royalist. He spent time on the Continent trying loyally, but ineffectively, to raise support for Charles.

How did he come back to Scotland?

The rebellion failed, but Alasdair MacColla was never subdued. When the smoke cleared Randal saw fit to recommend Alastair's services to fellow Royalists in Scotland. And so the next chapter begins. We've often noted that it is very helpful in telling a story to use names and faces rather than parties, factions or ideas. It's easy in this case as we have three clear main characters; MacColla, James Graham, Marquis of Montrose and Archibald Campbell, Duke of Argyll. Which of these are the good guys is up to yourself.

In early 1644 MacColla arrived in Ardnamurchin at the head of an irregular army. These were mainly Irish, veterans of the recent rebellion or former mercenaries seasoned on the Continent. Battle hardened! Scary! These were bolstered by a growing number of MacDonalds, and later soldiers from other clans.

They began raiding and plundering, mostly in Argyll. There was a justifiable suspicion that this was little more than a band of Irish pirates. In August MacColla finally met up with James Graham.

How was meeting Montrose so important?

James Graham was, in appearance, the epitome of a Cavalier; an honourable gentleman of culture and style. An unlikely partner to the unkempt Devastator, but it was a partnership that worked. For a while. He was Marquis of Montrose in Scotland's north-east. The north-east had been a hot bed of the king's supporters but James Graham was NOT among them! On the contrary, he had fought as a Covenanter in the Bishops' Wars. He was with General Leslie Alexander taking Aberdeen to put down this Royalism.

Quite what caused him to turn his coat is not clear. During an accord with Charles he was one of the Scots leaders who actually met with the king. Certainly he was one of those in the Scottish Parliament who opposed increasingly hard-line Presbyterianism. A personal animosity grew between himself and the leader of that faction. This immediately gave him a strong common bond with Alasdair MacColla. The man in question was the Marquis of Argyll, Archibald Campbell. For Alasdair, a MacDonald, hatred of the Campbells was in his genes.

Archibald had an early falling out with the king. On a visit to London he had been so bold as to tell him that his designs for the Church of Scotland were despotic – to his Royal face. Charles was not happy, but had little power to move directly against

Montrose.

Archibald. He did take measures that included reversing the previous royal gift of the MacDonald land of Kintyre, giving it back to the MacDonalds.

What does History remember?

Now these two, James Graham and Alasdair MacColla MacDonald, set out on an astounding run of military successes – a Year of Victories. So successful were they that James Graham has been rated as one of Scotland's outstanding military commanders. Some histories barely mention MacColla at all! To conventional history, Graham had all the requirements to be an army commander. He was a gentleman, with a title, from a family of recognised lineage. He had trained in the bona fide armed forces of the Scottish government under a well-respected general. He wrote regular letters to King Charles that can still be read. MacColla was a ragged-arsed highlander who had learned his skills among the bloody atrocities of the Irish rebellion. Who but Graham could be the brains behind the campaign? The Gaelic history tells a different story.

If you look at these battles, it is the very 'Highlandness' of the tactics that meant victory. These tricks weren't learned in Montrose!

The two met at Blair Atholl with a joint army that was growing as men of Atholl volunteered or were cajoled into action. They were bolstered by deserters from the government army.

The government army was hastily assembled to defend Perth. Perth is always strategic and it would give the Graham–MacColla force (the history books now define this as the 'Royalist army') a chance to stock up on supplies. The government force was largely made up of amateur conscripts. They assembled 3 miles outside of Perth; at Tippermuir.

How was the Highland Charge invented?

This is the first battle of the Royalist–Highland/Irish army and the idea of 'Highlandness' kicks in straightaway. Tippermuir is acknowledged as the spot where the 'Highland Charge' was invented.

The Highland Charge depends on three technical details of the matchlock musket; it is ferociously inaccurate except at very close range, it takes a long time to reload and it makes a lot of smoke.

The story goes that the Highland/Irish men were very short of ammunition. They held their nerve, advancing. The first volleys fired at them largely missed. Once those shots were fired there was so much smoke that the government troops could not see what was coming at them. Out of the haze (once they were close enough to 'fire into their beards') came a single volley from deadly close range. And the nightmare didn't stop; the Highlanders kept coming, abandoning their muskets for swords or turning them round to use as lethal clubs. The line did not hold! Nor did it at many future battles, right up until 1746.

The Highland Charge was invented!

It was, however, very similar to the tactics Alasdair MacColla had already used against English forces during the Irish Rebellion. It was also a framework that allowed the centuries-old Highland fighting style of personal valour and combat skills to fit into the new world of firearms.

Still James Graham got the credit. It is recorded that Graham gave a pre-battle speech. Apparently he said something along the lines of, 'Let not a musket be fired except in the very face of the enemy. Give but a single discharge, and then at them with the claymore, in the name of God and the King.' Battlefield speeches are very popular in retrospect (Elizabeth I's Armada speech is a cracking example). They are almost always made up afterwards – who among thousands of men would hear you? This was surely written by the Royalist propaganda machine.

How was 'No Quarter!' a very foolish command?

It is also recorded that Elcho, the government commander, yelled 'Jesus and no quarter!' If it was said, and if it was heard, this was an incredibly stupid setting out of the terms of engagement – in view of what happened next. In fact, you might say that had it been said and had it been heard it might be some sort of justification for what happened next.

The nightmare didn't stop; the government troops turned their backs and ran! The Irish/Highlanders didn't stop. It was said that you could walk on corpses all the way from Tippermuir to Perth without touching the ground.

How is the Drummer Boy to blame?

With neither the numbers nor resources to hold the town, Graham headed north-east looking for more recruits. In a short battle, with MacColla's men front and centre, they took Aberdeen. The story goes on that among the white flag party offering terms to the town was a drummer boy. A sniper from the walls shot the boy dead. This was the excuse for the atrocity that followed.

The War of the Three Kingdoms was a dirty war, with little chivalry from any side. Civilians suffered everywhere. Notable atrocities include the Parliamentarian siege of Colchester and Cromwell's sacking of Drogheda. The Drogheda affair has had more attention than others since the horror of it became ingrained in Ireland's psyche and made Cromwell a national bogeyman to this day. Recent historians have revisited the evidence and found (amazingly) that reports were exaggerated and it was really 'not that bad!'

In Aberdeen the troops did go on a spree of murder, rape and theft. A dead drummer boy was no excuse at all. But, as atrocities go (with civilian deaths somewhere between 100 and 200), it was 'not that bad!' By the time it hit the press in Edinburgh and London it was absolutely shocking. It proved two things; James Graham was not a fit gentleman to lead an army and those 'Highland bastards' were nothing but bloodthirsty barbarians.

The MacDonalds are coming!

What happened next smacked entirely of MacColla and his MacDonald Highlanders. Enmity between MacDonalds and Campbells was in the blood.

'Squinty' Archibald Campbell, 1st Marquis (also 8th Earl) of Argyll, was chief of Clan Campbell. Despite the fact that the Campbells' rise to power and influence was largely the result of support for Stewart kings, he now found himself in opposition to Charles Stuart. Despite his father's renouncement of Protestantism and return to the Church of Rome, he found himself as the leading champion of Presbyterianism in the Scottish Parliament. He was probably the most powerful man in Edinburgh – and the most powerful anti-royalist. He had supported sending the Scottish

Army south. Their contribution at the Battle of Marston Moor, and afterwards, swung the war in favour of the English Parliament.

He was outraged at the audacity of this mongrel army at Tippermuir and Aberdeen. He mobilised a second army to deal with them. But where were they?

They had disappeared into the Highlands. What Squinty Archie didn't know was that they were heading for Argyll to 'beard the lion in his den'.

BY THE WAY: The phrase 'beard him in his den' seemed very appropriate. The evolution seems to stem from 'there came a lyon ... I caught him by his beard' in the Book of Samuel, King James Version. To 'beard the lion' is used by Scottish writer Tobias Smollet in his book *Regicide – The Death of James I*, while the first appearance of 'to beard the lion in his den' is in Walter Scott's poem *Marmion – A Tale of Flodden Field*. So, a good Scottish heritage.

Squinty Archie.

Argyll is something of a natural fortress. In recent years the main approach has been blocked by landslides at the Rest and Be Thankful pass on the A83; in fact as we write this (in October 2021) it is shut, for the second time in a fortnight. If twenty-first-century motor transport can be halted at a mountain pass what chance would an army have? The only other way into the capital, Inverary, was by circuitous routes.

Furthermore, the Battle of Aberdeen had taken place in September. Military campaigns had been seasonal affairs, with armies laying up at the end of the summer. The idea of a winter assault IN THE SCOTTISH HIGHLANDS was ludicrous. James Graham knew that. Alasdair MacColla was of a different mindset. Historians, Johnston and Robertson, writing in *The Historical Geography of the Clans of Scotland* (1872) described it as 'the most daring and brilliant operation of the whole campaign – one of the most daring in all military history'. The credit goes to Graham, but it must have gone against every bone in his military body. For MacColla it seems to be merely typical. It was only imaginable with Highland knowledge, Highland survival skills and Highland fighting styles. How much more 'Highlandness' can you get?

A Merry Christmas!

Archibald Campbell was at home. The Campbells were totally unprepared when MacColla's army arrived by circuitous routes. They poured out of the winter hills into an undefended Inverary. Archibald and his family narrowly escaped by boat. The capital of Argyll was devastated.

The invaders must have had a merry Christmas at Campbell expense; they stayed until late in January, then tracked north across Rannoch Moor and Glencoe.

Archibald Campbell was not a happy man and he had the resources of the Scottish government behind him. Troops were pulled in from Ireland and some from the army in England. Favours were called in from northern clans.

How did the Great Glen Trap fail?

Graham and MacColla were heading for Inverness; travelling up the Great Glen. At Kilchurrin they learned that Campbell had a substantial army of experienced soldiers at the western end of the glen, behind them. They also learned that Campbell's allies had a second army led by the Earl of Seaforth at the eastern end, ahead of them. The Great Glen is a huge geological slash through some of Scotland's highest mountains; it is a string of deep cold lochs with precious little passable land along their shores. The steep sides were 'impenetrable!'. They were trapped.

As to what happened next? If the assault on Inverary through the Argyll hills was unexpected, this was madness. Over a thousand heavily armed men took to the hills in what was very little short of mountaineering. Climbing 2,000ft onto the slopes of Ben Nevis covering 36 miles in thirty-six hours – through the snow! Remember this was 1 February. Who but Highlanders would have attempted it?

They spent the night on the slopes of Ben Nevis and attacked at dawn – once again Campbell had no idea they were coming. The Highland Charge was once again a critical factor. In Graham's own words, 'Our men … came immediately to push of pike and dint of sword after their first firing.' Campbell's Covenanters ran, not that they had much option. Once again, as at Tippermuir and at Aberdeen, the Highlanders were relentless in chasing and slaughtering the fleeing men; a trail of bloody corpses. Graham even felt he should apologise to King Charles for it – 'we pursued for nine miles together, making a great slaughter, which I would have hindered if possible, that I might save your Majesty's misled subjects'. The Scottish government army was destroyed. Duncan Campbell of Auchinbreck, Archibald's leading general, was captured. Alasdair MacColla is said to have offered him beheading or hanging. When the Campbell complained that this was 'no choice at all', Alasdair took the top of his skull off with one sword swing.

Once again 'Highlandness' had brought the victory.

And Onward!

And the Year of Victories was not over. The year is 1645. Some of you will be aware of the run of Scottish victories in 1745 – exactly a hundred years later. In 1745 a leader, fighting for the Stewart monarchy, was strongly backed by Highlanders. They won battle after battle but after a time there was disagreement among his generals that changed his plans. This was followed by a catastrophic finale. This was, of course, Bonnie Prince Charlie. A century earlier there are some striking similarities.

In 1645 Graham and MacColla started with a spectacular victory at Inverlochy in February, followed by another big win at Auldearn in May and then again at Alford in July. In each case they suffered casualties described as 'light'. In each case the Highlanders ensured that enemy casualties were heavy, figures give about 1,500 dead covenanters. And there was worse to come – at Kilsyth.

Bloodier still!

Once again, on paper, the Covenanters' army looked good. Numbers recorded are notoriously unreliable, but certainly they outnumbered the opposition considerably. Plus the commander, William Baillie, had a second army of cavalry and foot, under the Earl of Lanark, on the way. Baillie planned to crush Graham's force between the two. It hadn't worked at Inverlochy and it didn't work now.

Baillie was hampered in that, as commanding general, he was not in charge – he had to answer to a committee. Running a battle by committee might not be sensible in the first place, but if it is dominated not by soldiers but by Presbyterian clergymen? Baillie's strategy was abandoned, and although he held the high ground with superior numbers he was destroyed. The battle was over before Lanark's force got close. The slaughter was repeated. Baillie and a body of cavalry were driven into a bog. Some figures give 4,500 dead; this was more than DOUBLE the number of Jacobites killed at Culloden.

The Winner!

James Graham, Marquis of Montrose, had won. Or had won Scotland! There was no one to oppose him. Bonnie Charlie never got anywhere close to having this amount of control over the country.

Graham rode to Glasgow and called a parliament in the name of Charles I. For a brief moment Glasgow was the capital.

James Graham had fulfilled his primary mission – to secure Scotland for the king and the Royalist cause, but he had never intended to stop there. He had always intended to cross the border to fight the English Roundheads. Events in England had overtaken him. A few months earlier, in June, the Royalists had lost again at the Battle of Naseby – this time decisively. Charles was on the run and trying, as usual, to talk his way out of it. Graham was told to stand down.

He ignored this and started planning an invasion force, but he had a problem. Alasdair MacColla MacDonald, for all that he may have been vaguely in support of a king of Scottish Stewart lineage, was first an independently minded Highlander and he was foremost a MacDonald. The hurt that he had done to Inverary last winter and the humiliation he had heaped on Archibald Campbell were good, but he had not achieved his prime objective of recovering former MacDonald lands, principally Kintyre, from the Campbells. He had no desire to travel to England to fight Roundheads. Furthermore, if he headed south he was turning his back on the Campbells, leaving the MacDonalds open to bloody retribution.

From 1 September 1644 to 15 August 1645 the partnership of James Graham and Alasdair MacColla had won battles at Tippermuir, Aberdeen, Inverary, Inverlochy, Auldearn, Alford and Kilsyth. A Year of Victories!

Now James Graham was on his own.

How did Montrose do on his own?

He made his way to the Borders hoping to pick up support and re-enforcements, without much success. He was forced into battle at Philiphaugh (possibly on the site that is now Selkirk rugby club). It was his first major fight without Alasdair MacColla. He was smashed!

To be fair, the opposition was better arrayed than before. The (First) English Civil War was pretty much over. The Scottish Parliament Army was holding station at Berwick and Newcastle. Sir David Leslie with 6,000 cavalry, dragoons and infantry, experienced men, came north. They caught Graham's army unawares. Despite a bold defence, a flanking manoeuvre by the Covenanters' superior cavalry tore them open. Graham was persuaded to flee.

The one Irish unit that had stayed with him, under Manus O'Cahan, had heavy losses. The last hundred surrendered under a promise of being given quarter. The Presbyterian ministers thought this too lenient; the men were executed along with 300 camp followers, including women and children.

James Graham finally got his song ...

Now let us a' for Lesly pray
And his brave company,
For they hae vanquishd great Montrose,
Our cruel enemy.

Ballad of Philiphaugh, Child 202

Philiphaugh has its own ballad, in Scots. Very pro-Covenanter. For songs of any of the other battles, you'll have to look to the Gaelic.

Graham headed north but failed to get support – he slipped away to Norway and then to France. He appeared again in Scotland with a few followers five years later. Landing in Orkney, he failed to rally any support from the Highlanders. He was betrayed by the MacLeods of Assynt.

Maiden.

He was beheaded by 'The Maiden' on 21 May 1650 in Edinburgh. Archibald Campbell is said to have been in the audience. His limbs were sent to Glasgow, Perth, Stirling and Aberdeen. His torso was buried in unconsecrated ground. His head was displayed on the 'prick of the highest stane' on the Old Tolbooth. The nation's highest accolade of dishonour; it stayed there for over a decade.

BY THE WAY: 'The Maiden' was Scotland's brutally efficient head chopping off machine. It was first used in 1564 during the reign of Mary, Queen of Scots. That was 228 years before the machine commissioned by Monsieur Guillotine was used in Paris. The author was perturbed to learn that the last person to receive the Maiden's blessing was JOHN HAMILTON in 1716.

Events in England led to a total turnaround in Montrose's post-mortem fortunes.

'Ne Oublie'

Bizarrely in a total reversal of Cromwell's post-mortem fate (buried with honour then exhumed for public execution), in 1661 once Charles II was in power, Graham's head was taken down, his limbs returned from their locations and his torso recovered from the paupers' graveyard. His various parts were laid in state at Holyrood before a splendid funeral in St Giles' Cathedral. The very place where the Covenant was born, and the mother-ship to the thousands of Covenanters that he slaughtered.

A splendid memorial was constructed in the cathedral (albeit in 1888). Above the statue is the Graham family motto *'Ne Oublie'*. How many people do remember James Graham, Marquis of Montrose and his role? His victories were outstanding and he might have been a Scottish national hero. Perhaps the fact that the foes he vanquished were also Scots had something to do with the fact he is largely forgotten.

'Nil Aoibhneas Fan Clan Domhnaill'

How many fewer remember Alasdair MacColla MacDonald, the man without whom Graham's campaign might have been very different? He never stopped fighting and his head was on the top of Archibald Campbell's wishlist. Alasdair drifted about the Highlands, then back to Ireland, where the Irish Confederate War was ongoing. He died, probably fighting, in some place, at some time.

As to his memorial? There is one. It's a small plaque in the small village of Clonmeen in County Cork, where he may or not be buried.

If you want a heroic, fearsome Highland rogue, someone to frighten the children with (especially if you are a Campbell), then this is surely your man!

KILLING A KING

Meantime, while Montrose and MacColla were having their adventure there were major events elsewhere.

Remember that clause in the Covenant about supporting the King of Scots? It is about to get kicked around a little. Charles I finally had to admit military defeat at the hands of the English Parliamentary Army supported by the Scottish Parliamentary Covenanter Army. Whether he remembered the clause or not, he felt his chances were better with the Scots and handed himself in to the Scottish Army at Newark.

How did the Scots sell their king to the English?

The Scottish Parliament then sold the King of Scots to the English. They did claim that they weren't selling a king, they were merely putting in an invoice for military services rendered. The First English Civil War was over.

During this period there was a major (complicated) religious stramash in England. The Puritans had gained power and they had much in terms of practice and belief to align with Scots Presbyterianism; they would seem to be natural allies. With the lid of the cauldron off, many conflicting ideas and aims boiled to the surface. In the thick of it one man rose from the steam – Oliver Cromwell.

Cromwell is a complicated character. He had learned quickly and proved himself to not only be a brilliant general, but also a charismatic leader to his troops. His New Model Army was disciplined, God-fearing and loyal, and he was driven by God's will – how could he be wrong?

Charles I had been brought up his whole life to know that he was appointed directly by God. How could *he* be wrong? Back in London, in comfortable custody, he set about negotiating his way out of the mess. Parliament and the Crown would have to come to an accommodation – he could see no option, and many in the Parliament could see no option either.

But, on the streets people were asking, 'What was all this suffering and bloodshed for if everything was going to return (more or less) to the way it was before?' A disgruntled population is not uncommon, particularly when they've been through a period of violent upheaval. This time was different; this time the grumblers included a very formidable army, with a very competent leader. The pot was on the boil.

How did the Scots support the King?
Charles escaped custody in London and England crashed into war again – the Second English Civil War. This time it was Cromwell and his army against Royalists and the English Parliament AND THE SCOTS.

In Edinburgh there was an argument for supporting their natural Puritan allies (alongside whom they had fought just a couple of years ago). But there was also an argument that Scots should defend their king, even if he had fought against them in the recent past. The king's supporters became known as 'The Engagers' and they gathered enough support to create a Scottish army to fight for Charles.

Opinion was split. The 'Kirk Party' opposed the agreement the 'Engagers' had made with Charles. The experienced army under David Leslie refused to join up. The 'Engagers' had a new amateur army with an amateur commander – the Duke of Hamilton.

Royalist risings in Wales and southern England didn't go well, so the Scots were meant to secure the north –Cromwell met them at Preston and had a comfortable win. The Duke of Hamilton was beheaded, alongside others, at Westminster. And that was pretty much it for the Second English Civil War.

How were Scots to blame for the execution of Charles?

What happened next was the well-documented trial and execution of Charles Stuart, King of England, Scotland and Ireland. The part that Scotland played was critical, if ironic. The Engagers had made an agreement with the King of Scots and had mustered an army to support him, BUT, looked at from an English point of view, the king of England had enlisted a foreign power (Scotland) to attack the 'good people of England'. Now, THAT was TREASON! It was exactly the stick (or axe) that Cromwell needed to beat him with.

On a chilly morning on 30 January 1649 **'The King of Scots was murdered by the English'**, at least that's how many Scots saw it.

Lang live the new King of Scots!

Given the events of the past few years and all the divisions that supporting or opposing Charles had caused, it was hardly simple. But many people in Scotland were incensed that their king had been killed and they hadn't even been consulted.

There was a sudden increase in support for the Stuart monarchy. Now the King was 'deid', 'lang live the king!', Charles II to be precise; he was declared King in Scotland and in Ireland.

Both kingdoms were out of order as far as the English Parliament was concerned. They had to be dealt with. Ireland was up first. Cromwell invaded and left a trail of atrocities in his wake, which are still alive in Irish memory. Politically, he turned the country upside down. The ruling class had been Anglo-Irish, who were basically Anglo-Normans, descendants of those that taken over the island in the twelfth century. They were, broadly speaking, pro-English, pro-Royalty and mostly still Catholic. They were stripped of their lands. Many went to exile in Europe; but they didn't disappear and they were not happy.

The new landlords installed by Cromwell, and in the years following, became the Irish Ascendancy and dominated Ireland until the twentieth century. Leaving half an army behind, Cromwell now set out to bring Scotland to heel.

Meantime, Charles II had landed in Scotland. He had been in France and latterly in Holland with his sister, Mary, and her husband, William of Orange. He was crowned King of Scots at the traditional coronation venue of Scone (unlike his father, who had been crowned in Edinburgh).

He was given a quick, though vigorous, education in all matters religious and had the duties and responsibilities of a good Protestant king drummed into him; he loathed every minute of it. The clause about supporting the king might still be in the Covenant, but so was the clause about defending the religion – support for Charles was strictly conditional. He had to swear to support the covenant. He had to promise to impose a Presbyterian church through all his kingdoms.

Charles wasn't happy, but this circuitous route was his best chance of getting back to London.

Cromwell is coming!

From the moment an agreement had been reached with the king, Scotland expected Cromwell. No doubt word of events in Ireland had slipped across. A plan was launched to muster a massive army in preparation, but it never reached the intended proportions. The clergy on the overseeing committee were determined that this was to be God's Army. In the first place, anyone who had any hint of association with the Engagers (who had supported Charles I) was ruled out. The army had the huge advantage of having David Leslie as commander, who had led Scottish troops to fight alongside Cromwell in the First English Civil War. He was an experienced general and held the loyalty of many who had learned from the experience of that campaign.

However, God's Army required its soldiers to be 'Godly Men'. Anyone tarnished by any form of bad language, drunkenness, lewd behaviour or any other misdemeanour had no place. But men who had fought though an essentially dirty war, who had witnessed and participated in some horrendous events were not all going to be angels – hundreds of hardened soldiers and many officers were sent home.

Leslie was not happy. Still he set about devising a strategy against what he knew well was lethal opposition. Given the record of Cromwell's New Model Army, the very last thing he wanted was to meet them in open battle. He employed a ruthless tactic. He 'scorched' Berwickshire and East Lothian, clearing the land of any food or supplies that Cromwell could use (hardly very beneficial to the local economy).

He let Cromwell march north, unopposed, as far as Edinburgh. The Scottish weather, not for the first time, came to the country's defence. The only chance the English had of getting food and supplies was by sea and they had occupied both Dunbar and Musselburgh for this purpose. Foul weather and raging seas blocked the supplies. By the time Cromwell was on Arthur's Seat (in Edinburgh) bombarding Leith, his army was already starving, riddled with dysentery and fever.

Despite constant pressure from the 'Committee', Leslie refused to be drawn into a battle; he preferred to send small raiding parties at night. The English withdrew to Musselburgh.

At this point Charles II himself turned up in the Scottish camp – a morale booster for the troops. The Committee was incensed, since they feared that loyalty to the king might overshadow the Godly mission of advancing the Covenant. The king was sent packing. They carried out a further purge of ungodly men and another eighty officers and 4,000 men were sent packing.

Cromwell had no choice but to turn tail and head 'hameward', it was all going right for Leslie. As Cromwell's weak and sickly troops trekked south they met Leslie's army. Depleted by the Committee, but still considerably more impressive than the English, the main force was in a strong position on Doon Hill, just south of Dunbar.

How did the Scots lose a sure thing?

Cromwell surveyed his situation. He had no way of bypassing the Scots. He had no way of attacking the Scottish position on the high ground. Yet, if he stayed where he was, without fresh supplies his army would disintegrate. He sent a hastily penned note to the governor of Newcastle (a Scottish victory would probably be quickly followed by an attack south). The letter, more or less said 'if we can't get them off that hill we're doomed!'

The Scots marched off the hill! By order of the Committee.

The Committee had been urging Leslie on to battle and a decisive victory for their Godly army: the Scots came down the hill and took up positions ready for battle on the morrow.

It is not clear whether Cromwell intended to simply blast a gap through the Scots and continue south or whether he thought he could, even with his weakened force, win a decisive battle. It is clear that he did not sleep; during the night he repositioned the various elements of his force. The Scots would have awakened to survey a completely different battle array from the night before, but he didn't give them that luxury. He attacked before dawn!

At 5 a.m. English cavalry attacked, catching the Scots still in their tents. In spite of all the strategic planning that had brought Cromwell almost to despair, the Scottish Army was caught by surprise. So battle commenced, but it was by no means a simple onslaught. Attacks were repelled and counterattacks launched. Fighting swung backwards and forwards. At the end of the day there was no doubt: the English had won. The surviving Scots had retreated to Haddington.

Around 5,000 Scottish prisoners were force marched (with a huge loss of life along the way) to Durham. There they were kept in appalling conditions in the cathedral – a recent excavation uncovered part of a mass grave. Many of these men were later sold into indentured servitude (close to slavery) in America.

Leslie's army was now defeated and severely depleted. Cromwell turned back north, making a priority of securing the Port of Leith and his seaborne supplies. He marched into Edinburgh. The castle was still occupied, but he took the time-honoured tactic of ignoring it.

A major defeat can have the effect of uniting and solidifying resistance, but in this case it did the opposite. There were plenty who blamed the Presbyterian hard-liners, their purges and urges. They tried to re-recruit the Engager supporters back into the rump of Leslie's army. The Hard-liners themselves took the opposite view – the defeat showed they had been abandoned by God because their efforts had not been hard line enough. They drew up a document, a 'Remonstrance', blaming everyone but themselves. They then tried to appeal to Cromwell, presumably on the grounds of their common fanatical Puritanism – he should leave Scotland in their hands. Cromwell treated them with distain and destroyed their hastily assembled army in a battle near Hamilton.

Charles II's Scottish army

Charles II and David Leslie tried to pull together a force including the remnants of his army from Dunbar, any Engagers that could be found and even some loyal Highlanders. (The 'pagan' Highlanders would have appalled the Edinburgh clergy.) They marched south. Cromwell's troops crossed into Fife, but kept the road south from Stirling clear. This might have been a deliberate plan.

On 31 July, Charles II led an army into England. A Scottish Army – a Scottish Army was marching to restore a Stewart to the English throne!

The plan was that all the English Royalists would immediately haul their swords from under their beds and their helmets from the top of their wardrobes and come marching merrily to Charles II's banner. It didn't happen. Any of this sound familiar?

After the Scottish army had gone south, mopping up Scotland was an easy matter, perhaps exactly as Cromwell had predicted. The Scottish Parliament surrendered two days after they left.

The Royalists, without any meaningful support, were caught and convincingly crushed in the Battle of Worcester, perhaps exactly as Cromwell predicted. (Almost) the last battle of the Wars of Three Kingdoms had been fought. The Stuart cause was lost.

Charles was on the run. Wearing a variety of disguises, he was shuttled about the countryside, with a hefty bounty on his head, just as Bonny Charlie would nearly a century later. Whether he ever dressed as a woman is not known. After six weeks he managed to get across the Channel.

Charles Stuart, uncrowned King of England, then spent some time living in some luxury as a guest of other European powers. Just as his nephew James Francis Stuart would do in the next generation.

He first stayed in France but due to politics was forced to leave. Despite his close relationship with sister Mary and her husband William, the Dutch (bizarrely) allied with the French and both allied with Cromwell's Parliament. Charles had to leave France (just like his nephew).

He took himself to Spain. Spain was exactly who Holland, France and now Cromwell's England were lined up against.

The Fourth English Civil War?

Charles had been trying to patch together a force from assorted Royalist exiles in France. In Spain he gathered further Royalists who had been serving with the Spanish; now he had some approximation of an army, always with the long-term object of invading England. In the meantime he was obliged to fight for his current hosts – the Spanish.

So once again a Royalist army went into battle with the Roundheads. This time on French soil at the Battle of the Dunes and once again it didn't go well for the Royalists. With huge losses to his amateur army, Charles II's plans for an invasion of England were out of the window.

In Scotland, Cromwell's general, George Monck, quickly took the major towns, including a brutal assault on Dundee. A major military presence was maintained to stamp out sporadic risings for some years. Scottish prisoners were exported as indentured labourers to North America and the West Indies.

Scotland abolished!

Two of the most significant dates in Scottish history are the Union of the Crowns in 1603, which left Scotland and England with the same monarch but their own Parliaments, and the Act of Union, 1707, which is in place to this day.

Less well remembered is the Act of Union of 26 July 1657: it effectively abolished Scotland. The Scottish Parliament was gone, and thirty seats in the London Parliament were assigned to Scotland. Governance of the country was overseen by a committee of eight English commissioners but matters on the ground were handled by the Military Governor, George Monck.

This was, of course, not the start of the United KINGDOM. There was no KING! This was the Commonwealth. The Commonwealth was the governing structure of the British Isles, but after Cromwell's death it started to fall apart. On 23 April 1661 Charles Stuart (II) was crowned King of England. It was all change – yet again.

The Commonwealth was abolished along with most of what it had enacted. The Scottish Parliament was reinstated: Scotland was back. It had, after all, crowned Charles King of Scots ten years before he was King of England. And it was time for retribution; the signatories to Charles I's death warrant were hunted down and executed – Cromwell's corpse was dug up and publicly executed.

In Scotland there were some recriminations, too. Archibald Campbell Marquis of Argyll, Squinty Archie, was found guilty of treason in Edinburgh, mostly for collaboration with Monck in later years. His head was removed by the Maiden. It was placed on the very spike that the head of his former nemesis, James Graham Marquis of Montrose, had just vacated.

THE KILLING TIMES

If I were to give you an image of Scotsmen fleeing across a heathery hillside pursued by Redcoats, you might think Jacobites after Culloden, but this is eighty years earlier. Those dying are not Catholic supporters of the Stuarts, quite the opposite. They are fervent Presbyterians persecuted by the officers of a vengeful Stuart king: they are Covenanters.

We noted, a short time ago, that many folk are confused as to who exactly the Covenanters were; simply, they are signatories to the National Covenant of 1638 or the Solemn League and Covenant of 1643. On a tourist visit to Edinburgh you might notice the monument to a hundred Christians martyred in the Grassmarket, or you may visit the Covenanters' Prison in Greyfriars Kirkyard. The latter is particularly ironic since Greyfriars was the location for the first signing of the covenant. These are also hundreds of incidents of random executions for crimes such as reading from the Bible – church ministers preached under pain of execution.

These stories tell of a heroic minority prepared to die in defence of Christian religious freedom. Martyrs! The Covenanters!

Wait a minute! Have we not been talking about the Covenanters for the last twenty-four years of Scotland's story? Covenanting Parliaments and (repeatedly) Covenanting armies?

Well, yes. From the signing of the first covenant in 1638 and the revised version in 1643, the Covenanters had risen to be the dominant political force in Scotland (or at least the Lowlands). They had fought both for and against Charles I. They had taken in the renegade Charles II, furnished him with an army and sent him south to claim the English throne.

Once Charles II was restored to the crown (in a period known as the Restoration) it was suddenly all change. Indeed, one of the first and most prominent of these heroic martyrs was Squinty Archibald Campbell, the very person who was being described as the most powerful man in Scotland just a few years earlier. This is very much Covenanters Chapter Two. This would be hard times for them; 'Killing Times' – they would last for twenty-eight years.

How much fun was the 'Playboy Monarch'?

Charles II is broadly remembered as the 'Playboy Monarch'; he was famed for parties and balls and frolicking with ladies. One of his biographers, Ronald Hutton described him, 'He was the playboy monarch, naughty but nice, the hero of all who prized urbanity, tolerance, good humour, and the pursuit of pleasure above the more earnest, sober, or martial virtues.'

Best known among his many ladies is Nell Gwynne, but the woman that fascinated him most was a Scot and a Stewart. Frances Theresa Stewart from Blantyre was christened 'La Belle Stuart' by Samuel Pepys and the king set his sights on her. Frances played the 'Little Miss Unobtainable' card and kept Charles at arms' length, which succeeded in fascinating him even more. To flatter her he had a medal cast with an image of Britannia sitting on a throne. When

Samuel Pepys saw the image he declared, 'There is Mrs Stuart's face as well-done as ever I saw anything in my whole life'. La Belle Stuart Britannia stayed on British coinage until decimalisation in 1971. And she is Scottish.

But Charles Stuart was not all sunshine and roses – there was payback. For those who had executed his father and kept him off his throne there were some pardons – but also a lot of executions.

How did he treat Scotland?

Scotland and its Covenanting Parliament had crowned him king a decade before England would agree it. They had raised an army to invade England and put him on the throne, but, they had HUMILIATED him. They had lectured him tirelessly about his duties as a Protestant king. They had made him swear to reorganise all his kingdoms into Presbyterian states. They had made him sign the damned Covenant. It was not forgotten.

He quickly renounced and denounced the Covenant. From 1661 he set a series of measures in law: the 'Rescissory Act' repealed all laws passed since 1633. The Abjuration Act was a formal legal rejection of the Covenant. It was declared to be 'against the fundamental laws of the United Kingdom'. The 'Oath of Supremacy' was still in place – dating back to Henry VIII – and declares the monarch to be the head of the church. Originally aimed at Catholics, it was also a statement that no Presbyterian could stomach.

He reinstated the bishops. Charles I had started the Bishops' Wars, which kicked off the Wars of the Three Kingdoms over just such issues.

The result was that Presbyterians were blocked from holding any form of office: the Kirk ministers were all excluded from their own parishes and could only get back by enrolling as one of the 'King's Curates', accepting the bishops and all the trappings of Episcopacy. Preaching outside the approved churches carried a sentence of DEATH. For the congregation, failure to attend approved services could result in heavy fines, deportation or execution.

The Scottish Privy Council authorised 'field executions' for those who refused to swear loyalty to the king and renounce the Covenant. Lynching for Presbyterians.

Who was 'Bloody Clavers'?

The government needed a strong man to carry out these harsh injunctions. They found one in John Graham, Laird of Claverhouse. To many in Scotland he became 'Bluidy Clavers' – a bogeyman. Children were bid to behave or 'Clavers'll get ye'.

Denied access to their own church buildings, ministers and their congregations took to the fields, holding open-air 'conventicles'. These were strictly illegal and were sought out; suspects were tortured to give up information. The gatherings were brutally dispersed – the preachers executed.

There are many, many stories of simple God-fearing folk meeting gruesome ends, but organised military resistance to this purge was (necessarily) very limited. There were various risings, but it was not until 1679 (seventeen years from the Act) that the Covenanters could claim a military victory – the Battle of Drumclog, such as it was.

A large open-air conventicle was held at Loudon Hill on the borders of Lanarkshire and Ayrshire with the Reverend Thomas Douglas preaching. Word came that Claverhouse's dragoons were on the way. This was not unexpected, so a number of the covenanters had brought weapons – some had muskets, others pitchforks. They had a few men on horseback.

They pulled back to a farm at Drumclog, where they took up position in a bog and opened fire on the approaching troops; the dragoons' horses couldn't charge across the bog. They were then surprised by a bold attack led by 18-year-old poet William Cleland. The troops fled; there was a story that Claverhouse's horse was injured and fled in blind panic, taking its unwilling rider with it. The troops followed their officer off the field.

It was a humiliating defeat for Claverhouse – there were thirty-six dead. (Do remember that at the Battle of Kilsyth just thirty years earlier the death toll was over 4,000.) It was not a big affair, but it was a victory for the Covenanters. Some continue to celebrate Drumclog as a victory for religious freedom.

The victory by those few hundred was a rallying cry. Three weeks later, 6,000 gathered on the banks of the Clyde at Bothwell Bridge.

There were enough now to be a real threat, but they had no organisation and critically no effective leadership.

The government forces were nearly as large and they were trained soldiers. The Duke of Monmouth (Charles's eldest bastard son) was brought up from England to take command. Claverhouse was in support.

The two forces were on opposite banks. The Covenanters tried to hold the bridge but after an hour they were driven back; Monmouth's troops poured over the bridge and the rest was a foregone conclusion. It is unclear how many were killed, but notably 1,200 were taken prisoner. Which takes us back to the tourist trail in Edinburgh.

The prisoners were marched to Edinburgh, where there were no facilities for such a large number. Greyfriars Kirkyard was commandeered and the Covenanters were held in the open air under armed guard. Conditions were appalling; many died, some were tried and executed, some escaped. In November the remaining 257 were loaded on to a ship bound for America as indentured labour. They didn't make it – the ship ran into foul weather off the Orkneys. The story is that the captain nailed the hatches shut as his insurance claim would depend on the loss of his entire cargo – even if that cargo was human. When the ship was ripped open on the jagged rocks a few men scrambled free. Forty-eight survived.

The period was called the Killing Times.

The persecution continued until the arrival on the throne of Mary Stewart and William of Orange.

the Anglican Church, of which he was nominally ... ...sted seven bishops, including the Archbishop ...

...pposition, headed by an unlikely partnership. James ...e of Monmouth, was Charles II's eldest son and might ...g except for the small detail that he was a bastard, or, ...ut a 'natural child'. He maintained all his life that his ... been secretly married (the evidence was hidden in ...black box). This would have made HIM, and not his ...doomed uncle, James II & VII. That would have made ... history.

...WAY: It is interesting, in a Scottish history, that ...h adopted the surname Scott (Stuart was denied ...ather than his unmarried mother's name Holt or ...ive parents' name Crofts. He took his wife's name. ...ott was a wealthy heiress and brought with her the ...e of Buccleuch (with major lands in the Borders and ...sshire). The Dukes of Buccleuch are his descendants ...ay.

...uth.

THE WILLIAMITE WARS

After the 'peace' of Charles II's reign we launch into the next war, which sees Scots fighting for a Stuart king in need of a throne. The plot involves the dispossessed Stuart, a royal bastard, a swashbuckling Scottish hero celebrated in song, a heroic victory and a brutal insult to the Highlanders.

It also introduces a new character – William, Prince of Orange!

How did Charles II leave a problem?

But back to the Stuarts. Charles II, the 'Playboy Monarch', had no problem with fertility. He fathered at least fourteen children, and by and large treated them well; they were not kept secret. The problem was that not one of them was with his wife, the long-suffering Henrietta Maria: he had no legitimate children – he had no legitimate heir. It may be to his credit that he didn't try any schemes to oust his unproductive partner, although there were some in English politics who would have been happy had he done so.

On Charles's death his siblings were then in line, namely his younger brother, James. Here comes trouble!

How was this James a recipe for trouble?

Charles was the Protestant head of the Protestant church in a Protestant country, at least in public. In a last act before meeting his maker, he converted to the Roman Catholic church on his deathbed.

His wee brother, James, had no such subtlety or (some would say) common sense. During the years of the Stuart exile he had been a guest of the French; there he had experienced Roman Catholic worship and converted, though he kept it secret for a decade. Now he was openly Catholic and it was resented by a great many. Nonetheless, in February 1685, he was crowned King James II, which automatically made him King James VII of Scotland.

He did know his way around Scotland as from 1680 he lived in Holyrood Palace, as Lord High Commissioner of Scotland, and had overseen the latter years of the Covenanter persecution. Traditional English history has dismissed James II & VII as a disaster waiting to happen, yet he did not start with an attempt to hurl the country headlong back into Catholicism, preferring to stand on a platform of tolerance for all, but then that's how Bloody Mary had started 132 years earlier and memories are long. He did begin a quiet campaign of promoting known Catholics to increasing positions of power in the military and civil life. He exhorted the Scottish Privy Council to be tolerant of Catholics and to intensify the persecution of Covenanters.

His first marriage to Anne Hyde was a love match; she was a commoner, not at all suitable for a Royal prince. In spite of opposition, they married in secret – although it was later made official. After her death, his second marriage to Mary of Modena, an ardent Catholic, sounded alarm bells, but concerns were mollified by the supposition that when he died the crown would pass to one or other of his Protestant daughters, and both had good Protestant husbands.

James VII.

How did a royal prince

James proved even more [...] twenty children (if you in [...] had proved good at produ [...] sons Charles, James, Edgar [...] had all died in childhood. M [...]

Unless James now produ [...] Mary or Anne would becon [...] also been fruitful, but equally [...] coronation she had, in additioi [...] borne a son and four daughter; [...]

Given the family record and [...] old age of 52 and his wife was [...] 15), a new son and heir seemed [...] would be no more than a footno [...]

Everything changed in 1688 [...] worse, to a son. Given how mu [...] 'royal birth denial' became the [...] elaborate and well-planned cam [...] prince had been stillborn or that [...] all; the live baby had been smuggl [...] bedpan. There were even elaborate [...] to show how the deception was ach [...] producing seventy witnesses to the [...] how important the event was. The c [...] Stuart, of whom more later.

the powers of [...] head. He arr [...] of Canterbury [...]

There was [...] Scott, the Duk [...] have been kin [...] more kindly [...] parents HAD [...] a mysterious [...] fractious and [...] for a differen [...]

BY THE [...] Monmou [...] to him) r [...] his adopt [...] Anna Sc [...] title Dul [...] Dumfrie [...] to this d [...]

CHARLES'S BASTARD

James intensified his appointments o [...] overturning previous legislation, such [...] been placed to hinder Catholics. He trie [...] inciting the courts (packed with his app [...] pronouncements superior to Parliament [...]

Monm [...]

His father denied his legitimacy, but still gave him titles and rank almost fitting for a prince, but not quite. No doubt the boy was aggrieved by the small detail that stood in his way. With a large part of the country growing less and less happy with the king, Monmouth saw his chance.

How was Archie Campbell Monmouth's man?

Monmouth had been born in Holland and it was from there he planned his campaign. It was there he met Archibald Campbell, Earl of Argyll.

The Duke of Monmouth was the guy sent north to crush the Covenanters and did so very successfully at Bothwell Bridge, and Archibald Campbell was the celebrated Covenanting martyr who lost his head to the Maiden in Edinburgh – but this wasn't Squinty Archie, this was his son – the 9th Earl.

Archibald Junior is an interesting character who seems to have suffered for being caught between two causes. He had been a young man when his father and the Covenanters had supported the restoration of Charles II and had marched south with the Scottish army that supported him. He was with Charles when he was roundly defeated at the Battle of Worcester.

When the king turned the tables on the Covenanters and executed his father, young Archibald stuck with the Royal side, which was the official policy of Scotland, and remained an officer in the king's forces.

He was not trusted, although he did carry out orders to harry Covenanters in Kintyre, but was criticised for being too lenient. On other occasions he was ordered to stand down as it was feared his troops might swing in favour of the rebel Presbyterians.

He met with the young Prince James during the prince's term as High Commissioner of Scotland. The prince must have seen a potential ally in the young Archibald as he offered him great power in Scotland, if only he would become Catholic. Archibald turned him down flat and made an enemy of the future king.

Archibald was caught in a bind; on the one hand he was a Royalist officer and had been a friend of King Charles II and on the other he was seen as a potential Presbyterian sympathiser on account of his

Archie og.

father. As a Scot he was compelled to swear an oath of adherence to Presbyterianism. His enemies (who included the 2nd Marquis of Montrose, the son of his father's arch enemy) seized upon this and declared this as treason to the king.

He was sent to trial in Edinburgh and found guilty; sentence was deferred for approval by King Charles. Charles, who was aware that killing a prominent Protestant would not be popular, allowed that the death sentence should stand but that it should be delayed at 'his pleasure'.

Archibald, jailed in Edinburgh Castle, did not trust the new King James to stand by his predecessor's word so he escaped. If you saw the scene in a movie you would probably think it clichéd. Archibald's young stepdaughter visited him, and since a young lady of stature could not go about the city unaccompanied, she was attended by a page. The page had, it was explained, met with an recent accident, hence his head and face was heavily bandaged. Stepdaughter and page left and, lo and behold, a servant was found, un-bandaged, in the cell – Archibald had escaped.

He flitted around England for a while, then took himself to Holland where he met up with Monmouth, who was in the midst of planning his coup against his royal uncle. Archibald ventured that he could lead a co-ordinated rebellion in Scotland, so at the start of May 1685 he set sail with a few ships and about 300 men.

How did Scotland have a Monmouth Rebellion?

For God and Religion, against Poperie, Tyrannie, Arbitrary Government, and Erastianism.

In Kintyre, a covenanting stronghold, Archibald declared that Monmouth was the 'Rightfu' King' and that Monmouth had the authority to reinstate his former title and privileges. He was looking for recruits, but while the Covenanters had plenty of reason for opposing James VII, Archibald's attacks on them a few years earlier were not forgotten. Of the few hundred men he managed to raise, most were Campbell kinsmen.

After a stopover on the Isle of Bute he made an attack on Greenock with no great effect, and then headed for Inverary. The area was already well garrisoned with government troops and the best he could manage was to seize Ardkinglass Castle on the shores of Loch Fyne. He retired to a castle on the small island of Eilean Gherrig. Under attack from two English frigates, many of his men deserted and he lost his ships as well as the castle.

An attempt to invade the Lowlands petered out after a few skirmishes with troops led by William Cleland (of Drumclog fame) he found himself on the run with just a few companions, including his son John. He was apprehended by militia men who had no idea who he was until he gave himself away by crying 'Alas, unfortunate Argyll!' He was handed over in Renfrew and taken to Edinburgh.

With the death sentence from four years earlier still hanging over him, there was no need for a trial.

Meanwhile, Monmouth launched his campaign in the West Country. The plan was to march triumphantly towards London enlisting thousands of disillusioned Protestant Englishmen as he went. It didn't happen. Many of those who did turn out were farm workers armed with nothing better than pitchforks. After a few skirmishes they met a regular army in the Battle of Sedgemore. The rebellion had lasted less than a month and the triumphant march had managed 40 miles.

How did Monmouth wish for the Sweet Maiden?

On 30 June 1685 Archibald Campbell, 9th Earl of Argyll, was executed at the Mercat Cross in Edinburgh, just like his father. On 15 July James Scott, Duke of Monmouth, was executed in London.

Monmouth might have wished he was in Edinburgh with his ally. Archibald lost his head to the brutal efficiency of the 'Maiden'. He referred to the machine as 'the sweetest Maiden I ever kissed'. In London, James Scott lost his to an incompetent axe-man who took six or seven swings and had to finish the job with a knife.

KING BILLY

King William III is one of the most recognisable British Royals to many, particularly in Northern Ireland. He is 'well kent' in parts of Scotland, too.

There is a problem with the Anglocentric interpretation of the accession of William to the throne of England; it is known as 'the Glorious Revolution' and also 'the Bloodless Revolution'. While his invasion of England might have been a walkover, events in Scotland, and certainly in Ireland were NOT 'bloodless'. Scotland and Ireland had the Williamite Wars.

How was Revolution 'Glorious'?

The next set of events largely happened in England, but they had major ramifications for what was about to happen in Scotland (and Ireland). Stuarts are heavily involved as both losers and winners.

James II & VII strengthened his standing army, promoting Catholics as officers, and continued his arguments with the Church of England. He went so far as taking a leaf out of his father's book and proroguing Parliament. It hadn't worked well for Charles I and didn't go well for James.

King Billy.

What about those two Protestant daughters? The elder was Princess Mary. As standard practice for a royal Princess she was married off to a Continental gentleman of acceptable noble standing and, hopefully, some strategic advantage for the king. Hence, she was shipped off to Holland.

Her husband was not exactly top-notch royalty, but he was the Prince of Orange from birth. His mother provided adequate credentials; she was Mary Stuart, daughter of Charles I, sister of James II & VII. Now her son, William of Orange, was marrying her niece, Mary Stuart, daughter of James II & VII. The couple were first cousins.

William had run a ragged road to become 'Statholder' of various states of the Netherlands – effectively, the ruler. It is sometimes necessary to enter English politics to tell Scotland's story, but we need not get into Dutch politics, except to say that it wasn't straightforward. He was an ardent Protestant whose greatest passion was his long-term enmity with the Catholic French, and Louis XIV in particular.

When disquiet about James's rule was raging it was inevitable that Mary's name would come up. A cabal of seven English gentlemen began writing to the Dutchman and a plan was hatched.

How did a foreign power invade England, without a shot fired?

On 5 November 1688 William of Orange INVADED England. This was no political or diplomatic manoeuvre, this was an armed invasion. He had over 400 ships with 40,000 men, including 11,000 infantry and 4,000 or 5,000 cavalry. This was a bigger force than William the Conqueror had brought back in 1066.

After the usual difficulties with the weather, the fleet arrived in formation at Torbay; flags flying, bands playing, volleys of musket fire. It was impressive! Once again the revolution was to start off in the West Country. His triumphal march got a lot further than Monmouth's. With a force of that size in good military order, with an artillery train of substantial cannon, James's army melted away, or turned their coats and joined William. Several of James's supposedly loyal supporters also defected, including his other daughter, Anne.

On 18 December William paraded into London with spectacular pomp and glory. William (who was not a handsome man) looked regal in full armour riding a white horse. In an age of propaganda, England (and London in particular) had been bombarded with bills assuring the public of William's goodness and, above all, his Protestantness.

James was already gone.

The queen and baby James Francis had left for France, with King James attempting to follow the next day. He had been abandoned by family, friends and, crucially, his army. In a fit of pique he flung the Great Seal, symbol of the king's power in the Thames. It shows how far he had fallen that when he was captured the next day, it was not by soldiers, or dragoons, or even militia – it was by fisherman. He was put into Dutch hands.

William had an anointed king as prisoner. He was all too aware how much trouble Charles I had managed to cause while imprisoned and how much upset had been caused by his execution. An absent king might be less bother than an imprisoned or headless one; that was pretty much how London saw it. He let James escape.

As William made his triumphant arrival in the city, James was escorted out the back gate by Dutch guards. Within a few days he was in France.

How did the English kick out a Stuart king in favour of a Dutch one?

An extraordinary 'Convention' Parliament was called and it decided that James's flight (plus the tantrum with the Great Seal) meant that he had abdicated and the Throne of England was vacant.

There was, of course a perfectly legitimate male heir in James Francis, but he was a child and he was not there. Instead there was a genuine Stuart princess to hand, Mary, and she came equipped with an apparently competent and Protestant husband in place. They got the job!

An unusual arrangement was installed in that they would be joint monarchs. Normally there would be a king and his marital consort or even a queen and her husband as prince consort (as worked for Victoria); this was to be equal King William and Queen Mary.

A huge problem for the Stuarts throughout their dynasty was that they could not abandon the notion of 'Divine Right': they had been appointed by God. While Mary had claim to the long royal history of her family, William had no such illusions. He was king by political appointment.

Parliament set about a raft of legislation including the pivotal 'Bill of Rights'. This enshrined that the king could not suspend laws passed by Parliament, levy taxes without Parliament, raise an army without Parliament, punish anyone who spoke in Parliament or interfere with elections to Parliament. Much of royal power and royal privilege were stripped away. William wasn't happy but he had other business with which to attend. It was the foundation of the constitutional monarchies of today.

It also included the rule that a British monarch could not BE a Catholic or MARRY a Catholic, which still stands.

England had had its 'Bloodless Revolution'.

BY THE WAY. Being unable to marry a Catholic severely the hampered the long-standing tradition of marrying royal offspring into the families of major European royalty. The Georges circumvented this by consistently marrying Germans. Until the current queen's father broke the mould they all married Germans (apart from one Dane). George VI, who had no expectation of being a king, married a Scot.

THE IRISH PART OF THE 'BLOODLESS REVOLUTION'

How did James VII come back?

In March 1689 James II & VII reappears. He turns up in Ireland with the French. Louis XIV was very in favour of monarchy, obviously, and very in favour of the Divine Right of Kings. He was also very opposed to William of Orange on political and personal levels. He was appalled by the Parliament-powered agreement that William had signed up to; helping James in Ireland made perfect sense. A French-backed conquest of Ireland would give Louis the platform of Ireland as a 'back door' to settle the ancient conflict of France versus England – and defeat William.

James could count on a generation of Anglo-Irish nobles who had been dispossessed by Cromwell. They were broadly pro-Stuart and mostly still Catholic. The administration, such as it was, remembered the Cromwell years. Ireland declared for James and not William and the United Kingdom.

There is a great deal to say about the three years of the Williamite war in Ireland. A great deal has been said and will continue to be said. Since this is a Scottish history, we'll try to be brief.

In the words of the song (yes 'The Sash') the events were 'Derry, Aughrim, Enniskillen and the Boyne'. The order is a matter of scansion rather than chronology.

In December 1688 James's forces approached the impressively walled city of Londonderry, which was a strategically useful site with a good harbour on Lough Foyle. They looked like they were going to waltz in without opposition until a gang of young apprentice boys slammed the gates in their face. The event is celebrated by the Apprentice Boys of Derry (not Londonderry) annually. The following spring James himself turned up, but he too was refused entry. This led to 105 days of siege with appalling hardship for those inside.

Enniskillen was a garrison town, a stronghold of support for William and an obvious target for James's troops. The matter was settled in a battle at nearby Newtonbutler; it was an early score for the Williamites.

The big one, in Irish memory, is the Battle of the Boyne. On 1 July 1690 William's international alliance won decisively and James fled.

The following year an even bloodier battle took place at Aughrim on 12 July 1691 – William wasn't present. When the calendar was rationalised in 1752, dates got confused and the Battle of the Boyne is celebrated on 12 July.

William's war in Ireland was, of course, more complicated than that; but he did win and James was back in France.

We have previously noted that it is helpful to have a nickname to help identify an individual rather than having to rely on name, rank and number. James Stuart, King James II of England and James VII of Scotland, got a nickname in Ireland. He was named *Seamus an Chaca* in Irish, on account of his general demeanour and the fact that he fled as soon as things started to go awry. It translates as 'James the Shit'.

THE SCOTTISH PART OF THE 'BLOODLESS REVOLUTION'

How was Charlie NOT the first 'Bonnie'?

Meanwhile, in Scotland we have a swashbuckling Scottish Jacobite hero for you with a great nickname, and a great song.

We have also a cracking movie scene to introduce him: a convention of dour old men in Edinburgh is sitting in a dull chamber, discussing Scotland's reaction to the events south of the border; King Billy's Glorious Revolution. When the discussion looks as though the meeting is going to support the immigrant Dutch upstart, William, a dashing young gentleman gets to his feet and eloquently defends the 'Rightfu' Stuart – King of Scots.

Dissatisfied, he storms out of the chamber, flings himself aboard a handsome steed and he rides, hooves clattering on the cobblestones, through the West Gate of the city. He is joined, in a clatter of horses, by fifty loyal dragoons. The guid folk of Edinburgh 'Hoorah!' and throw their bonnets in the air!

Come fill up my cup, come fill up my can
Come saddle my horses and call out my men
Unhook the West Port, and let us gae free
For it's up with the bonnets o' Bonnie Dundee

Welcome 'Bonnie Dundee'!

His name, rank and number was John Graham, 1st Viscount of Dundee. Viscount of Dundee was a new title conferred on him by King James in 1688, before that he was John Graham, 7th Laird of Claverhouse. Was that not the name of 'Bluidy Clavers' the bogeyman of the Killing Times? The same man. You do need to pick your heroes and villains carefully.

He was related to James Graham, Marquis of Montrose, of the 'Year of Victories', but that had been before he was born.

He had learned his military skills fighting on the Continent. He had fought with the French against the Dutch and with the Dutch against the French. There is a story that he rescued a young William of Orange on the battlefield, which may or may not have happened.

As for the events in the song? He did storm out of Edinburgh, but it was a month later that he raised the Royal Standard for James on Dundee Law – the gates of the city of Dundee were barred against him, so he went north. Once again the critical support for

Bonnie Dundee.

the Royal Stuarts came from the Highlands. The main mover was Ewan Cameron of Lochiel. Dundee requested re-enforcements and supplies from James in Ireland, but help was scant.

'The Braes of Killiecrankie – O!'

Things took a twist in Blair Atholl. Patrick Stewart, servant and lieutenant to the Duke of Atholl, seized Blair Castle in the name of James. John Murray, son of the duke, found himself besieging his own family home, with his own servants and neighbours inside. With Dundee and the Camerons approaching, Murray pulled out and joined the substantial government army advancing from the south, under General MacKay.

MacKay's army met Dundee (and the Devil) on 'the Braes of Killiecrankie'. Killiecrankie is a narrow pass, steep sided with the River Garry winding across the valley floor. Dundee was well placed when the opposition arrived, commanding the high ground on both sides. There were exchanges of gunfire but not much was achieved by either side, so it was not until eight o'clock at night that Dundee launched his attack. Once again the Royalist cause depended on the Highland Charge and it worked. The government line broke, the troops turned and fled.

It was costly for both sides; where the Highlanders came up against seasoned soldiers they had heavy losses. Many Camerons, perhaps 600 or more, were brought down by gunfire before they could raise their swords.

Bonnie John Graham of Dundee was again celebrated in song:

I met the devil an' Dundee,
On the Braes o' Killiecrankie, O!

It's a curious song. The narrator is on the Williamite side, admitting that:

It's nae shame, it's nae shame
It's nae shame to shankie-O [run away]
There's sour slaes on Athol Braes
And deils at Killicrankie-O.

There is no doubt that the song celebrates King Billy's worst defeat in his Scottish and Irish wars. It was a victory for the Stuart cause, but it didn't go so well for Dundee himself. In the latter stages of the battle he was struck in the chest by a musket ball. His much-quoted, but probably apocryphal, dying words went something like:

Dundee asks, 'How goes the day?' the reply is, 'Well for King James, But I am sorry for your Lordship.' Dundee answers, 'If it goes well for him, it matter the less for me.'

How much it mattered to King James is an open question. History did not find out if John Graham could emulate his kinsman's military success in the 'Year of Victories'. His replacements in command achieved little and many of the Highlanders went home.

Some skirmishes, such as an assault on Dunkeld, were both costly and pointless. The only other event that graduated to the level of 'a battle' at least has a song. It would hardly be remembered without it.

The Battle of Cromdale was a disaster for the royalist forces. They were only saved from even worse carnage by a heavy fog that shrouded their retreat.

The song 'The Haughs of Cromdale' is a peculiar one. The fifth verse reports:

But, alas! We could no longer stay
And o'er the hills we come away
Sair we did lament the day
That e'er we come to Cromdale

This is fair enough. The song then goes on:

And the loyal Stewarts, wi' Montrose
So boldly set upon their foes
Laid them low wi' Heiland blows
Laid them low on Cromdale

The song resurrects Montrose, who had been dead for forty-four years and has him defeat 'twenty-thousand Cromwell's men'.

Bearing in mind that Cromwell had been dead for thirty-two years, this seems an unlikely turn of events.

Be careful where you get your historical information from – even The Corries!

'Deep is the snow'

Cromdale was the end of the major military opposition to the ousting of James VII, but there was another incident that looms large in Scotland's memory. The fact that it has a great song helps.

Sporadic resistance did flare up, mostly in the Highlands. William was frustrated by this as it was a distraction from his main focus against the French, requiring troops that might have been on the Continent.

An amicable solution was proposed; Highland chiefs were offered sometimes substantial financial incentives to sign an oath of allegiance to King William and Queen Mary. Lord Stair, from Ayrshire, had the task of implementing it – the problem was that Stair did not trust the Highlanders, MacDonalds and Camerons in particular.

A closing date for acceptance was set – 1 January 1692. The Clan Chief McDonald wrote to James, on behalf of the other Chieftains, asking permission to sign, unless of course he could launch an invasion before that. He could not and did actually send a reply giving permission. The letter arrived with the chief of the Glengarry MacDonalds, but he did not pass on the information until 28 December; this gave some of his fellow chieftains a very tight schedule for signature.

MacIain, chief of the small Glencoe MacDonald family, duly set out on 30 December and presented himself in Fort William; he was told that he should have gone to Inverary. He turned round and headed for Argyll with an official note for the Campbell magistrate in Fort William to authenticate the fact that he had turned up on time, if in the wrong place. His paperwork was completed on 2 February. But he had technically defaulted and Lord Stair was delighted.

He wrote in a letter, 'My Lord Argyll tells me Glencoe has not taken the oaths at which I rejoice ...'. This follows on from previous letters that had stated that he wished to 'destroy entirely the country of Lochaber, Lochiel's lands, Keppoch, Glengarry and Glencoe ...' and 'their chieftains all being papists, it is well the vengeance falls there'. He was looking to set an example.

The Glengarry MacDonalds were late too, signing on the 4th. Their lands were confiscated on paper and then returned later. For Glencoe the repercussions were more 'practical'.

Robert Campbell from Glenlyon, with around 120 soldiers, arrived in Glencoe at the end of January. The locals were expected to provide accommodation and food, which was a fairly common imposition in lieu of taxes.

It was not Stair's intention to deliver a slap on the wrist. A further 400 troops were assigned to join Campbell in an assault of 'fire and sword'. In addition, another 400 men were to arrive at the head of the glen to block the escape of fleeing MacDonalds. He was sending an army against a small, undefended rural settlement.

After two weeks as guests (albeit uninvited), Campbell received orders. They came, not by messenger, but in the hand of Captain Thomas Drummond, a superior officer. There may have been some doubt as to whether or not Robert Campbell would actually carry out the command. The order was to execute their hosts.

The killing began and 13 February will be remembered for the 'Massacre of Glencoe'. Captain Drummond personally shot some of those who pleaded for mercy. MacIain died with around thirty kin, including women and children, while others escaped to die on the mountainside.

It was all over by the time the government reinforcements arrived, although they did carry on burning their way up the glen. The troop that was to block the refugees arrived late and MacIain's sons escaped.

Oh cruel is the snow that sweeps Glencoe
And covers the grave o' Donald
And cruel was the foe that raped Glencoe
And murdered the house o' MacDonald

The massacre was appalling enough to become an obvious propaganda weapon and the reports did force an enquiry. The enquiry recognised that since the order had been signed by King William himself there was no question that the enterprise had been totally legal. The only matter to be challenged was whether the officers had overstepped the mark. They suffered no great repercussions.

In the Gaelic world it was a huge matter: news of it rang through the Highlands. The Clans, however barbaric they seemed even to Scottish Lowlanders, lived by long-held traditions. Rights and obligations were ingrained in the culture and one such rule was hospitality: people were duty bound to receive visitors, even from another clan, to refuse was unacceptable. To abuse that hospitality and turn on your hosts was a cultural abomination.

It was a small affair, militarily, but it evokes strong emotions still.

QUEEN ANNE AND
THE END

…it will gang wi' a lass

At the start of the new century the monarchy was in a bind. King William died in March 1702. Once again there was no heir. There was always James II & VII's other Protestant daughter, Anne; she was crowned queen the same month.

Her problem was that she was only going to be a stopgap as she was already 37. Any hope that she would leave behind a Protestant male heir were dashed when her only surviving child, William (the potential William IV), died at the age of 11, two years earlier. She had suffered a further sixteen pregnancies with no happy result and was plagued by ill health, not surprising given her natal history. A new child (even in a bedpan) was not expected. The first question on the agenda from day one of her reign was 'What happens when you die?'

She must have known that she might possibly be the last reigning Stewart/Stuart, fulfilling the prophecy of her great, great grandfather. James V, lying on his deathbed in Falkland Palace, said of the Stewart dynasty, 'It started with a lass and it will gang wi' a lass.' He was both wrong and right. He was thinking the end would be with his daughter Mary (who was Queen of Scots from the moment he closed his eyes).

It ended with Anne 172 years later, although that decision would shortly be contested.

History has been very unkind to Anne, not least in the 2019 movie about her. Her character was blackened by the memoirs of Sarah Churchill, the Duchess of Marlborough, her former chief lady in waiting and close friend. After a fallout, Churchill delivered a tirade of what historians today regard as scurrilous fiction, but this was the story that was told in history books (and the 2019 movie; by the way, there were no rabbits).

How was Queen Anne HUGE in Scottish history?

People might not think of Queen Anne as a hugely important figure in the story of Scotland, but we have been, throughout this book, trying to judge how they CHANGED Scotland.

Anne is MASSIVE!

She might not have been the chief architect of the events that occurred but it happened on her watch, and she did play her part in making it happen. She changed Scotland forever.

When Jamie Saxt, James VI, became James I of England, his dearest ambition was to unite the two kingdoms and consolidate his power base, but he failed. He was canny enough to not waste his new feather bed in the attempt. Queen Anne succeeded!

Against all expectations, Anne turned up at her first address to Parliament looking good. She delivered a bold and confident speech and in that speech she stated that it was 'very necessary' to have a union between Scotland and England – her great grandfather's precise wish. She got it!

Queen Anne.

In England she is remembered through Queen Anne furniture and Queen Anne architecture. Her reign saw a flourishing of artistic, literary, scientific, economic and political advancement, which many Scots chose to embrace.

Empire and enlightenment

Anne came to the throne in 1702 at the beginning of a new century. The seventeenth century had been very much a game of two halves, with the second half being one of the most brutal periods in Scottish history. It was as much torn by internal conflict as by external foes.

So what of the eighteenth century, the age of enlightenment? It certainly started on a military footing with the Europe-wide War of the Spanish Succession and then the Napoleonic Wars. When they ended in 1815 with the Treaty of Paris it would be almost a hundred years before there was a major Continental war.

In Scotland recollection of the century focuses on the next phase of the Stuart Wars. Namely, the exploits of yet another James and another Charles Stuart – the Jacobite Risings. But before we can get to those there are some issues to consider.

A few years before there was the incident of 'the Scottish Empire'.

THE SCOTTISH EMPIRE?

The whole enterprise of empire really kicked off in the reign of Queen Elizabeth when England joined France, Spain, Holland and Portugal in the business of seizing chunks of the globe, subduing the natives and exploiting them for every drop of resource they could squeeze. They then had to spend considerable effort defending them against their fellow plundering nations.

Through the centuries England had shown tendencies towards expansion. They had ongoing claims on France, or parts of it, and constantly pushed their claims on Ireland, Wales and Scotland.

Scottish leaders had, on the whole, been content to regard

Scotland as the whole pie (apart from occasional attempts to co-opt Northumbria and Cumbria).

At the end of the seventeenth century the rewards of the exploitation of foreign lands, in terms of plundered resources, international trade and global influence was clear to see. Why should Scotland not have a go? A plan was hatched. It certainly did not lack ambition.

What was the plan?

The scheme, dreamed up by William Paterson, was not a tentative venture to set up a small trading company; it was, in his own words, 'the door of the seas and the key to the universe ...'. The vast resources of Asia and the Orient could only be reached by sailing way south and then east around Africa's tip, the Cape of Good Hope or way south and then west around the tip of South America, Cape Horn. Both journeys were long and highly treacherous, where risks were high and costs were huge.

By contrast, the Atlantic crossing from Europe to the Caribbean was well known and familiar. If you could unload your goods and transport them across a short causeway and load them on another ship in the Pacific Ocean your risk would be lessened and your costs lowered. In Paterson's words:

> The time and expense of navigation to China, Japan, the Spice Islands, and the far greatest part of the East Indies will be lessened more than half, and the consumption of European commodities and manufactories will soon be more than doubled.

It was a fantastic prize. Paterson had touted his scheme across Europe seeking backers but getting no takers, but now the Scots, it seems, were ready for an adventure. What could possibly go wrong?

It might have been wise to have considered who it was going to be upset. The Spanish was the obvious answer. Since 'discovering' the 'New World' they had regarded the Southern American continent as their own personal fiefdom and deeply resented any intrusion. The expedition carried cannon, muskets and pistols to repel a Spanish attack.

Darien ship.

What the 'Company of Scotland', which was set up to administrate the scheme, failed to take into account was how much it would upset the English. It upset England politically as it was managing a fragile relationship with Spain. If a war with Spain was to blaze they didn't want the fuse lit randomly by some foolhardy Scottish adventurers.

Worse, it upset England commercially, particularly through the lobbying of the East India Company. The company became hugely powerful, acting almost as an independent nation state wielding its own fleets and armies. They were to effectively conquer India. They were the biggest bullies in the playground of the Pacific and this scheme could undermine their existing infrastructure. They opposed it and so as a result did the English king and government.

It was asserted that the Company of Scotland had no legal right to seek funding abroad. English bidders were forbidden from supporting the scheme and (since King William was still powerful at home) so were the Dutch. The money had to come from Scotland and Scotland alone. And it went well. Mr John Holland, a London merchant, stated, 'When I came down to Scotland, I found Mr Paterson very popular ... and I found the whole nation universally in favour of the Indian and African trade.'

The prospect of high returns was so well assured that £400,000 was raised in a few weeks and the game was on.

The adventure begins

In July 1698 five ships sailed from the Port of Lieth, sailing around the north of Scotland to avoid British ships. They carried, in addition to the weapons and the usual supplies of biscuit and salt beef, considerable quantities of claret and brandy. They also carried 'Scotch Hats, a great quantity; English Bibles, 1500; Periwigs, 4000, some long, some short; … made of Highlanders' hair'. They brought lots of small mirrors, combs and trinkets to trade with the simple 'savages'.

On board were 1,200 souls. Many were ex-military men, including Captain Thomas Drummond (the chap who was at Glencoe on THAT 13 February). There were 300 'gentlemen volunteers', younger sons of the gentry, seeking their fortune. Many did not know where exactly they were headed – that was a secret.

Darien is situated on the thin umbilical strip of land joining the South and North American continents. Today it is part of Panama. It is a region of jagged peaks, mangrove swamps and sub-tropical rainforest – to this day much of it has no roads, so that the 'Darien Gap' is referred to as the missing link of the Pan-American Highway. The climate and terrain was highly dangerous to any European; to peely-wally Scots it was deadly.

The expedition arrived in November and the natives were friendly, at least at first. They loathed the Spanish (with good reason) and supported any opposition to them; however, they were not impressed by combs and mirrors and brought little food to trade.

Good progress was made constructing a harbour settlement – New St Andrews. Work began on a more permanent home – New Edinburgh. Disease struck and they started to run out of food as much of the rations they had brought were spoiled. King William had forbidden any of the English or Dutch in the Caribbean to supply them. Disease raged and the settlers fell out with each other and factions formed.

I'll not go into detail; there are plenty of good sources if you enjoy a harrowing fiasco. After seven months the remnants abandoned Darien; of the 1,200 who set out, around 300 remained alive. They limped to Port Royal on Jamaica, but because of the embargo sent from England they were refused entry. A few, including Paterson and Drummond, made it to the small port of New York. When they learned that two supply ships were on their way to Darien, Drummond commandeered a sloop and headed back.

The supply ships reached Darien and found it deserted. One of the ships caught fire and was abandoned, as disease hit the crews. They headed for Port Royal, but they were also turned away.

Meantime, back in Scotland, a few early letters had made it home, beaming with hope and confidence. No word of the disaster had got through, so the second fleet was on its way.

With over a thousand people on board, four ships sailed from the Clyde. Perhaps suspecting that the settlers may not have had all the skills required for surviving in a hostile jungle, the Church of Scotland stepped up and sent clergymen, four of them.

The ships arrived a year after the first expedition expecting to find a thriving prosperous community. Instead they found the hulk of the burned-out supply ship and the remnants of Drummond's New York crew skulking among the ruined huts.

There was discord from the start. Many of the new settlers expected to join the bustle of New Edinburgh, not build jungle huts from scratch. Arguments broke out, preparations were neglected and within a couple of months the long-awaited Spanish arrived. After a month blockading the harbour, the Spanish gave an ultimatum, surrender or expect a major assault with 'no quarter'. They surrendered. The Darien venture was over.

The repercussions in Scotland were huge. Figures vary widely but certainly a very significant portion of Scotland's entire capital was lost. It was said that there was hardly a family (of note) that was not hit – Scotland was bankrupt.

QUEEN ANNE'S SUCCESSOR

Since before William's death, the politicians in London had been spending their time poring over family trees and genealogical charts trying to find the nearest living individual with legitimate Stuart blood. They found candidate after candidate but each had to be rejected. The problem was that the Stuarts and Stewarts before them had gone with the traditional path of royalty and married off daughters and younger sons to other royalty across Europe, and very few of these families were Protestant. Now, going down the list, they found Catholic, after Catholic, after Catholic. It was enshrined in law that the monarch could not be Catholic. Fifty-seven candidates were rejected.

They ended up with Sophia of Hanover. The lady was electress of an obscure state within the Holy Roman Empire, not even a country. But she was Protestant, admittedly Lutheran Protestant, so she may have been more comfortable with the Scots Presbyterian worship than the Anglican Church that she was being invited to govern. She was near enough.

Her dynastic credentials were good. She was the granddaughter of James I himself. Had James's daughter Elizabeth not been overlooked because of her sex we might have had her as British monarch instead of her wee brother Charles I. We know how he turned out!

Instead, she married King Frederick V of Bohemia. She had a daughter, Sophia, who was being asked to stand by to take the English throne. I say 'English Throne' because the Scots had other ideas.

King William had been personally involved in her selection. The English Parliament enshrined the decision in law in the Act of Settlement before Anne even sat on the throne. Sophia wouldn't live long enough – instead it was her son, George, with all the other Georges to follow.

'THE END OF ANE OULD SANG'

Scotland was reeling from the Darien Disaster. Not only had many influential individuals lost heavily, but the economy as a whole was damaged. The failure could be laid at several doors, but one clear perception was that England had not only failed to support the scheme, they had opposed and hindered it. One conclusion was a simmering resentment, but another was an understanding that Scotland could not perform on a global stage without England's help and the way to get that may be a closer relationship.

How did Scotland threaten England?
Either way, what Scotland needed was some leverage. The succession crisis seemed an opportunity, so the Scottish Parliament passed the Act of Security, which restated that Scotland had the right to decide on its own monarch. The threat was that Scotland would choose some other Protestant candidate other than the one England chose. Anyone! Which would bring an end to the Union of the Crowns.

How did England threaten back?
The English may have recognised that Scottish national pride is not to be ignored, but it is a fickle beast. They certainly recognised that Scots had vulnerable pockets. In retaliation they passed the Aliens Act. This meant that Scots would be regarded as foreign aliens in England, with no right to trade in England or in any British colony on the face of the globe.

If the English response to Darien was an open snub, this was a kick in the teeth. It effectively shut down most of Scotland's exports at a stroke. It was an opening shot in a now blatant campaign to draw Scotland into union; it was a mean stick, but there were carrots, too.

Negotiations took place in London with the Scots and English delegates meeting in separate rooms, passing proposals on paper back and forth. Given Scotland's previous threat, the acceptance of the Hanoverian succession was non-negotiable – Scotland was getting the Georges.

How was Scotland 'bought and sold'?
In terms of national economies Scotland's was small but fiscally sound – there was no national debt. England, on the other hand had a national debt running into many millions of pounds. This rather esoteric financial imbalance provided justification for flinging money at Scotland. The sum, known as 'the Equivalance', was £398,085 10s sterling, with over half of it going to those who had lost money in Darien.

There was an additional slush fund of £20,000 for payouts to noble gentlemen who were also voting members of the Scottish Parliament. The Duke of Queensbury, who was London's chief promoter of the YES vote in Scotland, managed to keep more than half of this for himself. There were also titles, positions and pensions up for grabs.

Who were the 'parcel of rogues'?

The Court party within the Scottish Parliament were actively supporting the Union. There was also a group of political firebrands calling themselves 'The Squadrone Volante', the 'Flying Squad'; they must have thought themselves a real wild bunch. They could be persuaded. They included James Graham, 4th Marquis of Montrose. He voted for the Union and the Hanoverians, and his great grand-father's various bits must.have been rattling in their coffin (he was promoted to Duke on the back of it).

Some including Andrew Fletcher of Saltoun, John Hamilton, Lord Belhaven and the influential Duke of Hamilton argued against. The Duke of Hamilton, however, did not turn up on the day of the vote. He had toothache, which apparently can be quite unpleasant, and there were others who were absent.

On 16 January 1707 the Scottish Parliament voted away Scotland's sovereignty and voted itself out of existence by 110 votes to 69.

Nearly every commentary on these events quotes the Robert Burns lines about 'English gold' and 'Parcel of rogues'. Here is the full poem:

Fareweel to a' our Scottish fame,
Fareweel our ancient glory
Fareweel ev'n to the Scottish name,
Sae famed in martial story
Now Sark rins over Solway sands
An Tweed rins to the ocean
To mark where England's province stands –
Sic a parcel o rogues in a nation!
What force or guile could not subdue
Through many warlike ages

Is wrought now by a coward few
For hireling traitor's wages
The English steel we could disdain
Secure in valour's station
But English gold has been our bane –
Sic a parcel o rogues in a nation!
O would, or I had seen the day
That Treason thus could sell us,
My auld grey head had lien in clay
Wi Bruce and loyal Wallace!
But pith and power, till my last hour
I'll mak this declaration
We're bought and sold for English gold –
Sic a parcel o rogues in a nation!

The bells of St Giles in Edinburgh, on the day the Union came into effect, played a tune called 'Why am I so sad on this my wedding day?'

The recently promoted Earl of Seafield, now Chancellor of Scotland (a YES voter), said: 'There's ane end of ane auld sang.'

THE JACOBITE RISINGS

How was the Jacobite rebellion not a rebellion at all?

It is surprising how many people who would consider themselves pro-Jacobite freely use the terms the 'Old Pretender' and the 'Young Pretender', when this is clearly a calculated insult. It casts James Francis Stuart and Charles Edward Stuart as outsiders 'pretending' to the throne: they were anything but.

James VI & I took the English throne on the grounds that he was heir to the Tudor line through his grandfather's marriage to Margaret Tudor, daughter of Henry VII and Elizabeth of York. The Stuarts were also legitimate descendants of the Plantagenet line through James I's marriage to Joan Beaufort, who was great granddaughter of Edward III. Further, all Scottish monarchs since Malcolm Canmore are descendants of the ancient royal house of Wessex thanks to Malcolm's marriage to Margaret, daughter of Edward the Exile.

If there is such a thing as 'royal blood', it flowed in Stuart veins.

If you believe at all in royal 'lineage' and the rule of primogeniture (succession of the oldest male) then James Francis Stuart was legitimately James VIII of Scotland and James III of England.

In which case the Jacobite 'Rebellions' were not 'rebellions' at all, rather it was the supporters of the Georgians who were 'rebelling' against the 'Rightfu' King'.

After his failure in Ireland, James VII retired to a chateau (and it was no humble cottage) as a guest of the French. He had with him his surviving son, James Francis. James Francis grew up in the certain knowledge that he was rightfully a king, he just needed to bang a few heads together to make it so. On his father's death he was recognised as King of Scotland by France and Rome and some in Scotland.

'NOW OR NEVER' – 1715

There were various plans to bring the Stuarts back – the 'Fifteen' was the one that should have worked. In Scotland the ill effects of the Act of Union were biting deep and causing huge resentment. In England, George I was newly on the throne and he was not liked; his personal demeanour and the fact that he made little effort to speak English – and the fact that he preferred to spend his time at home in Hanover – did nothing to endear him. If ever there was a moment this was it.

Charles Francis was led to believe that 'five in every six Englishmen wanted a restoration'; it was 'now or never!'

What about the English rising?
What is not often recalled in the Scottish story was that reclaiming Scotland was merely Plan B. Plan A was to seize the West Country, with James sailing in from Le Havre to a secure Plymouth with 2,000 troops. Supplementary actions in the north and in Scotland were not much more than an afterthought.

The leaders gathered at Bath under the pretext of a race meeting, but the secrecy surrounding the rising was deeply flawed. When alerted that the government was on to them, they melted away, although several were rounded up and sent to the Tower of London.

On 6 September John Erskine, 6th (and also 23rd) Earl of Mar raised the Stuart standard at Braemar and things started well enough; they took Inverness, Aberdeen, Dundee and Perth – although a raiding party failed to take Edinburgh Castle. Mar hesitated, allowing the Georgian (or Hanoverian) forces to organise. These were led by a Scot, John Campbell, 2nd Duke (or 11th Earl) of Argyll.

By this time Mar had around 22,000 men across the country, a bigger army than Charlie would have in 1745. Mar headed for Stirling with about 4,000 and met the enemy in the Battle of Sheriffmuir. The Jacobites still outnumbered them by about three to one – it should have been an easy victory.

Who won the Battle of Sherriffmuir?
The Battle of Sherriffmuir was a game of two halves. Essentially

Mar's left won while his right was driven back by Campbell. Mar typically dithered; he failed to commit his forces to following up the opening that had been created, he let the Georgians drift away to fight another day. Both sides claimed victory, but both sides had a lot of casualties.

It was captured by Robert Burns in 'The Battle of Sherramuir'. The poem, based on a contemporary report, has two shepherds retelling their contradictory versions of the day. One says …

> The great Argyle led on his files,
> I wat they glanced twenty miles;
> They hough'd the clans like nine-pin kyles,
> They hack'd and hash'd, while braid-swords, clash'd,
> And thro' they dash'd, and hew'd and smash'd,
> Till fey men died awa, man.

While the other …

> O how deil, Tam, can that be true?
> The chase gaed frae the north, man;
> I saw mysel, they did pursue,
> The horsemen back to Forth, man.

1715 banner.

Meantime, Scots were also fighting in an action to take the north of England. It came to grief at the Battle of Preston.

Mar had failed to push ahead when he had the impetus, he had split his forces, and he had failed to secure a win when he had the advantage on Sherriffmuir. He may have drawn the battle but he had lost the war.

When James Francis arrived in Peterhead on 22 December he was already beaten. The Georgian forces had quickly beefed up their forces and brought in heavy artillery. The Jacobites were forced back and their soldiers faded away – in February James sailed back to France.

What about 1719?

James continued to hawk his cause around Europe. He had another go in 1719, this time supported by the Spanish, rather than the French. Again the main focus was to be the south-west of England and 5,000 Spanish troops were expected to land. Meantime a Scottish force, with a much smaller number of Spanish soldiers, was landed by Spanish ships in the Hebrides. They had brought arms for 2,000 men. They gained some support from the clans, but not enough. The remaining weapons were stored in Eilean Donan castle, where they were seized by the Royal naval forces.

The venture came to an abrupt end at the Battle of Glenshiel. The Georgians had superior firepower, including mortars. It's said that the Highlanders slipped away under the cover of smoke from the burning heather, abandoning their Spanish colleagues.

The landing in Devon never happened as the Spanish were driven back by a storm (again).

THE BONNIE PRINCE

James Francis had been forced to relocate as the English had demanded his expulsion as part of a treaty with the French. He travelled to the Papal States and was given the Palazzo del Re (Palace of the King) in

Rome. It was here that his sons, Charles Edward Louis John Casimir Sylvester Severino Maria Stuart and Henry Benedict Thomas Edward Maria Clement Francis Xavier Stuart, were born. Their mother was Maria Clementina Sobieski of the Polish Royal house.

Charles Edward would go on to become one of the best-remembered Scots of all time – Bonnie Prince Charlie. He spent less than a year of his life in Scotland, yet his memory is celebrated in hundreds of songs in Gaelic, Scots and French. His image has appeared on millions of shortbread tins, tea towels and tea cups.

> BY THE WAY: In 2009 art historian Bendor Grosvenor revealed that one of the most frequently used images of Charlie was actually a portrait of Charlie's brother, Benedict Stuart. Grosvenor then went on to discover the real portrait of Charlie, painted by Allan Ramsey in 1745 in Edinburgh, in a gloomy corridor in the home of the Earl of Wemyss. The image used here is the 'right' one.

Like his father, he was brought up in the certain knowledge of his royal status. The throne of England was the prize and Scotland could be a stepping stone.

Prince Charlie.

> BY THE WAY: His father considered bringing him up as
> a Protestant to make him more acceptable to an English
> audience. It didn't happen.

As he came of age he started campaigning on behalf of his father. The big hope was for support from France to stage a military intervention and then the good folk of Great Britain to welcome the Stuarts back with open arms.

How was Charlie to get support?

Who exactly was going to support the Stuarts is a complex question. In England there was a good deal of resentment towards King George. Among the landed gentry (the folk who had fought as cavaliers in the previous generation) many would be happier with an old-school monarchy. There was still a Catholic minority who hoped for advancement.

In Scotland the big issue was still the Union. It had been a very raw issue back in 1715 and it hadn't gone away. The concentration of wealth and power in the south-east of England was resented. Nothing much changes! A Catholic restoration was not on the cards, but the Episcopalian church might gain ground against the Presbyterians under the Stuarts.

As for the Highland clans, some were Catholic, but not all. The clans had been in conflict, on and off, with the Stewart and Stuart kings of Scotland for centuries. The new style of centralised British government left them on even more of the periphery than before. They were under economic and political threat. Another factor, especially for the MacDonalds, was the centenary of the 'Year of Victories' when they had defeated the 'government' forces again and again – this could be a chance to relive past glory.

How did Scotland nearly turn Charlie away?

The possibility of an attack through Scotland was being discussed; Jacobite sympathisers met at the 'Buck Club' in Edinburgh – opinion was divided. Murray of Broughton was among those who urged caution. A vote was taken and a letter drawn up: it told the prince that unless he came with 6,000 troops, arms for 10,000 more and 30,000 Louis d'Or in cash, he was bound to fail.

The letter was entrusted to another Charles Stuart, 5th Earl of Traquair. The earl was distracted by a visit to his mistress and turned up in Edinburgh four months later with the letter still in his possession. Another messenger was sent, but by that time Charlie had left Paris.

THE FORTY-FIVE

With vague promises of support from the French at some point down the line, Charlie arrived on Eriskay on 23 July 1745 on the French ship *Du Teillay*.

> The news from Moidart come yestreen
> Would soon gar mony ferlie
> For ships o' war had just come in
> And landed royal Chairlie
> Come through the heather, around him gather
> You're all the welcomer early
> Around him cling, wi' all your kin
> For **wha'll be king, but Chairlie**?

How did Charlie not bring 6,000?

He didn't bring the 6,000 men requested – he brought seven. Seven men that is – two Scots, one English and four Irish. They are celebrated as the 'Seven Men of Moidart'.

Less than a month later comes one of the celebrated moments in '45 mythology – the raising of the standard at Glenfinnan. It was reported that the hordes of Highlanders: 'threw their bonnets in the air and huzza'd ... crying aloud, 'Long live King James VIII and Charles, Prince of Wales. Prosperity to Scotland and no union.'

It was actually a bit of a damp squib, but over the next few weeks clan warriors trickled in.

In order to stage a solid takeover of Scotland the strategy had always been to set about securing as many of the key towns and castles as possible: Perth, Aberdeen, Inverness, Dundee and critically Stirling. Bruce had spent years doing it. But holding Scotland was not on Charlie's agenda, he went straight to Edinburgh.

He rode into town to huge hoorahs and the tossing of bonnets. It was here that the ladies of Edinburgh gave him the revered title 'Bonnie'. He took up residence in the Royal Palace of Holyrood (as a bona fide prince should). His tactic in regard to Edinburgh Castle was to ignore it; he didn't need it, he had control of the streets.

Twas on a Monday mornin
Right early in the year
When Charlie came to our town
The Young Chevalier. Charlie is my darlin, my darlin, my darlin,
Charlie is my darlin, the young Chevalier.

He issued two proclamations. One annulled the Act of Settlement, which banned his Catholic father from the throne, the other was to dissolve the Act of Union, a top priority for much of his Scottish support, 'the pretended Union of these Kingdoms being now at an End!'

The first major battle was at Prestonpans. By now Charlie had 5,000 foot and 500 horse – a mixed force of Highlanders, Scots regulars and Irish (the French contribution was to send Irish soldiers who had fled to France). George Murray was given overall command, while Irishman John O'Sullivan (one of the 'Seven Men') was at Charlie's side.

General Sir John Cope was the government's man in Scotland; surely he could be expected to deal with this rabble? King George's son, the Duke of Cumberland, was off fighting in Flanders; there was no need to recall him.

Cope had comparable numbers, but many were untrained recruits. He met the Jacobite army in full battle and the battle lasted FIFTEEN MINUTES! The government army turned and fled.

Hey, Johnnie Cope, are ye wauking yet?
Or are your drums a-beating yet?
If ye were wauking I wad wait
To gang to the coals i' the morning.

General Cope, in his court martial, would complain, 'the manner in which the enemy came on was quicker than can be described'.

Charlie's army had been underestimated. Cumberland got his wish and was recalled from Flanders along with 12,000 troops.

Charlie, given the diverse aims of his supporters and his troops, could not hope to command by 'Divine Decree' – he had to deal with committees. He pressed for advance to England.

The conventional (expected) way was to strike down the east coast (but General Wade was in Newcastle); instead they hit Carlisle. It was a substantial fortress and Charlie had no means to have a prolonged siege, but it capitulated quickly – it was a good win of arms and supplies.

They marched on through Preston and Manchester and arrived in Derby. Now was the big committee moment. They were within 150 miles of London, and there was panic on the streets of the capital. Charlie was confident that as soon as they got close to looking like winners the English Pro-Jacobites would turn out in force AND the French would weigh in with real support rather than vague promises.

The Scots were not so sure; they had done their bit. Once they crossed the border the English Jacobites were supposed to rise up and carry the weight, but that hadn't happened.

They were dodging TWO English armies, one under General Wade and one under the Duke of Cumberland.

George Murray was pragmatic; if they engaged and WON, they would be so depleted in men and arms that they could not complete the campaign, while if they LOST, then not a single Scotsman would make the long journey home alive. O'Sullivan and the Irish had nothing to lose and supported Charlie along with some of the Highlanders.

Then Dudley Bradstreet turned up with fresh intelligence. There was a THIRD army, recruited from the streets of London, standing between them and the city. It would hold them up while Cumberland and Wade piled into them from behind.

Bradstreet was a government agent. There was no 'Third Army', but it swung the argument and Charlie turned back north. The campaign was not going to be won in a single bold sweep. But once the troops were home in Scotland they could regroup and win a longer war.

He met government troops again in (another) Battle of Falkirk and won. Since he had neglected to secure any Scottish strongholds, much of Scotland was hostile – he made a belated attempt to take Stirling without success. He was forced further north.

The Duke of Cumberland had arrived in Scotland. On 15 April 1746 both sides were camped near Inverness; a battle was imminent.

That night Cumberland's troops were issued a ration of brandy to celebrate the duke's birthday. What better plan than to launch a night attack than against a woozy enemy?

The Jacobites set off in the dark in two parties; the going wasn't easy and it took longer than anticipated. George Murray decided that it was too late for the attack and turned back. The message failed to reach the second team and the two groups passed each other in the night. When Charlie's troops reached the rendezvous there was no Murray and they turned back. It failed to achieve anything other than to exhaust the men. And the next morning was the big event.

CULLODEN

The Battle of Culloden is one of the most celebrated battles in Scottish history. It was a major disaster, but Scots do like a heroic defeat.

Jacobite commanders have been criticised for picking the wrong battle ground. Murray and O'Sullivan each chose a site, but neither was happy with the other's choice – in the end it was immaterial. No one chose the spot, it was just where the forces ended up in the morning.

How was it not all fearsome Highlanders?

A very popular perception of the Battle of Culloden was that brave heroic tartan-clad Highlanders, armed only with swords, were overwhelmed by ranks of trained muskets and cannon fire. The evidence, supported by recent battlefield archaeology, is that the Jacobites delivered a formidable amount of 'fire' but what really swung the day was the British cavalry armed, ironically, with swords.

There is a common perception that Charlie's army was all fearsome Highlanders, which was exactly what the Georgians wanted you to think. Perhaps the most well-known image of Culloden shows Redcoats facing off against unkempt kilt wearers or the force of law and order against 'thieving Catholic Highland bastards'. The portrait (by David Morier) was commissioned by the Duke of Cumberland!

The Georgian propaganda programme was desperate to promote the idea that the entire rebellion was about the irrational claims of a bunch of dissatisfied barbarians. What right-thinking man could identify with such nonsense? This idea ignores the fact that the Highlanders were only a part (albeit a significant part) of the forces on the day, in the campaign and in the ongoing Jacobite struggle. It was a much more convenient idea than dealing with the complex motivations of the many people in Scotland, England and the Continent who were unhappy with their regime!

Culloden.

Who were Charlie's Army?

There were Highlanders in Charlie's army; MacDonalds of Clanranald, Keppoch and Glengarry, Camerons, Stewarts, Frasers, Mackintoshs, Farquarsons, MacLachlans, MacLeans, but more than half the soldiers were from the Scottish north-east and Lowlands. Plus there were Irish, French and even a few English. Even among the Highlanders most men were armed with up to date French and Spanish muskets and they were well drilled.

Cumberland had sixteen battalions, four of which were Scottish including the Campbells of Argyll. He did have more cannon and mortars and, critically, he did have more cavalry.

On the uneven ground the Jacobite charge didn't go as planned. The centre veered into the right and the left were slowed by boggy ground, while the fire from the Hanoverians was relentless. Parts of the Jacobite line got through and delivered considerable mayhem, whole others failed. Cumberland had held back his cavalry until the Jacobite structure had broken down, then sent them in to do their bloody work.

The whole thing was over in an hour. Charlie was forced off the field by his companions, much to his chagrin – he wanted to charge again.

Prince William Augustus, Duke of Cumberland, third son of King George II, had beaten Prince Charles Edward Stuart, son of King James VIII of Scotland – both men were aged 25.

The 'Forty-Five' was over.

ON THE RUN

For Charlie there followed five months on the run: for some part sleeping in the heather, mostly secreted into loyal households. There is the much-told story of Flora MacDonald disguising him as Betty Burke, her maid. Finally, he made it to Skye and away to France.

Speed bonnie boat, like a bird on the wing,
Onward, the sailors cry;

Carry the lad that's born to be King
Over the sea to Skye.

If you want to remember Prince Charlie as a romantic hero there is
every reason to. He arrived in Scotland with seven men and he defied
the might of the British state for a year. He won every round, but got
'gubbed' in the final. He was always the underdog, but he put up a
fine fight. He must have been a young man of considerable charisma
to inspire the loyalty he clearly did.

On his father's death he was NOT recognised internationally as
heir to the thrones, as his father had been. If you want to remember
the hero Prince Charlie then do not research his later life. It is not a
happy story. Just listen to the songs.

What happened to the army?
Around 1,500 survivors gathered at Ruthven Castle, but they
received orders from Charlie to disperse, as did other Jacobite units
that had missed the battle. The Highlanders might have been able to
slip into the hills and maintain a guerrilla campaign, as Bruce and
Montrose had, but for most of the troops this was not an option.

The Duke got his nickname 'Butcher Cumberland' more from
the aftermath than the battle itself. Wounded men were killed on the
battlefield and in the days and weeks following.

Prisoners were not slaughtered wholesale, as some have claimed.
Captured nobles were sent for execution in London. Of the common
soldiers, a proportion stood trial (the prisoners may have drawn lots
among themselves); of those tried about 120 were executed, many
more were deported into 'penal servitude', while most of the rest of
the men were released.

What if Charlie had won?
If Charlie's expectations had been realised and English Jacobites had
risen then there is every likelihood that Britain would have been
flung back into the horror of the civil wars of the previous century.

Since James VII left England there had been Kings William and
George, both appointed by Parliament – the idea of an all-powerful

monarch had been consigned to history. The Jacobites were not really campaigning against the fat Georges – they were against the British State. Overthrowing that would not have been easy. If it had happened, the history of Britain might have been very different.

For Scotland it would have meant a return to a shared monarch and a devolved Parliament – Scottish independence had never been on the agenda.

The failure of the rising did have significant ramifications for Scotland, particularly the Highlands.

Culloden and the Highlands

The British government were very keen to blame the entire Jacobite rebellion on the Highlanders. Sandhurst military historian Christopher Duffy stated as recently as 2003, 'I have made a point of asking professional historians at random about their impression of the Jacobite forces … With slight variations in wording their answer has inevitably been: "thieving Catholic Highland bastards". The aims of the rising could not surely be promoted by any right-thinking Englishman or Scotsman.'

Since the fault had entirely been theirs, retribution must necessarily fall on the Highlanders. And it did. Scotland in general, and the Highlands in particular, were subject to a sustained period of military occupation as efficient as any imposed by the Normans or even the Romans.

Much of the Highlands was difficult to access, much of it was unmapped. Map makers were not welcome – some lost their heads.

> BY THE WAY: There is even a story that a map maker was staked out naked on an island in Loch Maree and left to the midges!

William Roy took on the task and produced 'Roy's map of Scotland', which was at the time the most accurate map of any part of the British Isles.

General George Wade had already started building decent roads to allow the military to travel swiftly and the task was completed by

William Caulfield. Much of the road network of today is based on their plan.

Fort William and Fort Augustus were upgraded. A brand new state-of-the-art fortress was created at Fort George. British garrisons were imposed on communities up and down the country.

BY THE WAY: In the Highlands Fort William has always been referred to 'An Gearasdan' – THE Fort They had no wish to celebrate the Dutchman. At the time of writing there is an active campaign to drop the 'William' from the town's official name.

There was a deliberate attack by legislation; the extent of the military occupation made this feasible. There was the Dress Act followed by the The Act of Proscription 1746.

This act describes itself as 'an act for the more effectual disarming the highlands in Scotland; and for the more effectual securing the peace of the said highlands'. To this end it aimed to pull the Highland beast's teeth:

it should not be lawful for any person or persons to have in his or their custody, use, or bear, broad sword or target, poignard, whinger, or durk, side pistol, gun, or other warlike weapon …

It was also an attack on education. As the Act notes, 'it is of great importance to prevent the rising generation being educated in disaffected or rebellious principles'.

And to this end, 'obliging the masters and teachers … and chaplains, tutors and governors of children or youth, to take the oaths to his Majesty, his heirs and successors …'

The best-remembered part of this act is the attack on culture, particularly on the dress code:

And be it further enacted … that no man or boy, within that part of Great Briton called Scotland … shall on any pretence whatsoever, wear or put on the clothes commonly called Highland Clothes (that is to say) the plaid, philibeg, or little kilt, trowse, shoulder belts, or any part whatsoever of what peculiarly belongs to the highland garb; and that no TARTAN, or partly-coloured plaid or stuff shall be used for great coats, or for upper coats.

There was no specific mention of bagpipes. Banning Gaelic might have been thought desirable, but it would have been unworkable.

How were the clans attacked?
Another act in the same year was arguably far more important – the Heritable Jurisdictions Act, 1746.

The Highland clans had been living under a clan system that recognised the land as being the communal property of the clan members. The clan chieftain was the chief executive officer. The clansmen had obligations to the chief and the chief had power to be judge, jury and executioner if need be, but he also had responsibilities to defend and provide for his flock.

The Heritable Jurisdictions Act took away these powers: but it also took away the obligations. Much land had been confiscated and was now offered up for sale. The very rock and soil of the Highlands was now a commodity – it could be sold and bought.

Remaining clan chiefs quickly discovered that under the new feudal-style regime they were no longer the guardian of their lands – they were the OWNER!

They could have said, 'Wait a minute, this is not the system here,' but they didn't: they grasped it with both hands.

> BY THE WAY: The Act was also a curtailment of the powers of the other Scottish nobles. Those that had supported the government were compensated. The likes of the Duke of Argyll and the Duke of Hamilton got big cash payouts.

This attack was an attack on the very structure of the clan system. It changed the Highlands forever.

CLEARANCE

Much of the Highlands is agriculturally marginal; the Straths, the valley floors, could stand up to a little cultivation, oats for porage and little else – but the mountain slopes were fit only for grazing and cattle was the currency. The land did support a much bigger population than it does today, although the standard of living was not palatial.

Now that it was under new ownership, or a different style of ownership, it was looked at as a business proposition. The people could be squeezed for rent, but not much – there was no spare money. Much of the local economy was in barter.

Even for the former chieftains there were new incentives to get cash. They were aspiring to the degrees of opulence they saw in some of the houses of nobles in other parts of Scotland. They were sending their sons to England for a proper education. They wanted to mix with those they would like to see as equals; they wanted to entertain and be entertained and it all cost money.

The new owners had no relationship to the land or people. Estates were bought as an investment and investment needed to make a return. Penniless tenants did not pay the banker.

The remnants of the Caledonian Pine Forest were not destroyed by demand from any war or other threat; it was defeated by economics. Cheap imports from the Baltic made Scottish timber unprofitable, so no effort was made to replant. There are still places in the Scottish landscape where ancient Scots pines stand, well-spaced; these were left as 'seed trees', but their seedlings would not be allowed to thrive.

Sheep were the valuable commodity; there was a demand for mutton and the wool price was buoyant. The Highland hills were summer grazing, but to make the enterprise work required the Straths, which were the places where the people lived. The people had to go!

The process, known as the Highland Clearances, started in the years following Culloden and would go on for a century.

Entire communities were uprooted and moved. Many were settled on the coast, where some estates tried to create new industries; fishing and kelp burning. These may have provided a modicum of income to the people, but the profits were going to the estate.

Some landowners encouraged (and some even paid for) emigration to the New World. Others opposed it, seeing the feeble population as an asset to be used in money-making schemes.

Some unfortunates were cleared once, then cleared again as the owner's priorities changed.

The system of crofting was developed for the displaced. Some people have a romantic idea of the Highland croft, but it was designed to be a piece of ground where it was impossible to make a living. For a family to survive they needed another source of income – that meant working for the estate or going elsewhere.

Often the fit men left in search of an income. The crofts were managed by old men, children and women. And what were the young men to do? What they had always done – FIGHT!

'THERE WAS A SOLDIER'

The Highlanders HAD proved themselves to be a formidable force for centuries – the 1745 campaign was no exception. The concept of the ferocity of the Highland soldier was well established.

It was logical for the British government to recruit these young men into British regiments. It not only filled the ranks with men born into a long-standing martial tradition it also removed them from Scotland. Andy Stewart's song from 1961 was perceptive, the key line being 'soldiered far away'.

> There was a soldier, a Scottish soldier
> Who wandered far away and soldiered far away
> Andy Stewart, 1961

BY THE WAY: Andy Stewart's song was not only a chart hit in the US, it was also a number one in Canada, Australia and New Zealand. The tune came from a pipe march that was originally a chorus part in Rossini's opera, *William Tell*.

The process was already under way. General Wade's measures after 1715 to 'civilise' Scotland included the recruitment of Highlanders into militia to 'watch for crime' – they became known as the Black Watch. Ten of these groups were then formalised as the 43rd Regiment of Foot in 1739. During the '45 rising they were kept well clear of Scotland as their loyalties were not entirely trusted; this was not least because they had mutinied two years earlier at the prospect of being sent overseas. They were unhappy at being commanded to London, claiming they had only enlisted to serve in Scotland, but were assured that the trip was only for a royal inspection. On arrival they were directed to the Channel ports, where they were further incensed by a rumour that they

Scottish soldier.

were being sent to the West Indies. It was believed (correctly) that there they were likely to fall victim to any number of tropical diseases. They marched for home, but were soon turned around. Their officers were court-martialled and shot and the men sent to Flanders. A few years later the Black Watch did find themselves in Jamaica.

Who were 'the ladies from Hell'?

After Culloden, and for many generations to come, signing up for the British army was a better option than any that existed at home. The proud tradition of British Highland regiments was born. They became key to British success in the numerous wars of colonisation. Very often they 'soldiered far away'.

Ironically, at the time of the Act of Proscription the only situation in which a Highlander could legally wear his native kilt was as a member of the Georgian army. The kilt became such a feared military emblem that it was later foisted on Lowland regiments.

Kilts were in full use as combat dress right through the First World War. Scots in the trenches were nicknamed 'the ladies from Hell'. They were abandoned early in the Second World War. Except for pipers.

What of those left behind?

For the population left behind there was not a lot of good fortune. Economic schemes, such as the kelp industry, that had provided at least some sort of income, collapsed. Potatoes had replaced oats as the main form of nutrition and the Highlands was hit by the same potato blight that had devastated the peasant folk of Ireland.

BY THE WAY: Many people agree that is more appropriate to call the events in Ireland 'the Great Hunger' rather than 'the Great Famine', since Ireland had no shortage of food. It was exporting oats, barley, wheat, butter, beef, mutton and pork. But none of it was available to the suffering class.

Emigration continued as Australia had opened up as a destination. Men who had served in the military abroad and gained a little land sent for their families.

Even sheep were failing to provide the hoped-for rewards. Debt among the landowners was common to the extent that over 60 per cent of estates changed hands in the first half of the nineteenth century. Any residual connection between the landowners and the land was being washed away.

Then in 1842 Queen Victoria and Prince Albert visited the Highlands, inspired by the queen's love of the writing of Walter Scott. Six years later they bought the Balmoral Estate on the banks of the River Dee. Hunting, shooting and fishing was in high fashion and the Highlands were the place!

> Everybody who was anybody in 1850 wanted a Highland sporting estate. There were plenty of takers in the Victorian world of burgeoning industrial capitalism – an emergent class of nouveau riche, redolent with competitive snobbery, desperate to emulate a traditional land-owning aristocracy.
>
> John Lister Kaye

Not much has changed. A survey in 2002 found that 66 per cent of estates were owned by absentee landlords and 61 per cent had been purchased rather than inherited.

The Highlands had been 'bought and sold for English gold' (though in recent years the nationality of the buyers is more diverse).

SCOTLAND
THE NOO!

WHO'S TO BLAME?

The narrative of this volume draws to an end in the aftermath of Culloden. Scotland was now an integral part of the United Kingdom of Great Britain and Northern Ireland: it was governed from London. Only in the final year of the twentieth century did it get back a Parliament, albeit with limited powers.

But to round this book off and take it back to where it started there is one more date that needs to be explored – 1822. It features a king – King of England (and King of Scots) – George IV, but the architect of the events is the man to watch. If you want to ask who is to blame for the international perception of Scottish culture then there is a prime candidate.

The King Georges had been constitutional monarchs: Parliament was the power. They were pre-occupied by petty family squabbles and had clung to their German heritage as much as their British (they all married Germans). In general they were not afforded much respect by their subjects. They were routinely mocked in the popular press.

Meantime, Britain (including Scotland) had seen a period of relative prosperity. The benefits of empire were becoming apparent. Industrialisation was emerging. The middle class were on the way up (by 1832 they would even get to vote).

George IV was described both as a 'charming sophisticate' and a 'degenerate boor'. He was 57 when he finally got the crown in 1820.

He set off on a tour of Ireland. He made all sorts of popular promises that he had no power to keep. It went very well. He was cheered in the streets.

In 1822 he launched his 'charm offensive' in Scotland. He was in Edinburgh for 'one and twenty daft days'. It went well and it changed Scottish history.

This story left the Highlands devastated in the wake of Culloden. Tartan was banned (although this had been repealed). All things Gaelic were persecuted. The landscape was being cropped short by Cheviot sheep. The people were banished from their homelands, shifted from one scene of poverty to another.

But suddenly, in 1822, while the Highland clearances were in full swing, Gaelic culture (or rather a facsimile of it) became high fashion – BY ORDER OF THE KING!

WALTER SCOTT

Major changes are rarely the work of one individual, although this book has often chosen a figurehead, rather than the actual complicated array of contributors, to tell the story. In this case one man has to take a lot of the credit – or the blame: Sir Walter Scott.

Walter Scott was related to the Walter Scott who had turned coat on his former allies in the borders on behalf of James VI, but he was by no means a noble; he was born in Edinburgh's Old Town. As a child he suffered from polio and was sent, for the good of his health. to stay in the borders with his granny. There he became engrossed in oral stories and song.

Back in Edinburgh he studied law – he made his first trip to the Highlands as a clerk to oversee evictions.

His literary career started with translating German poetry. At the age of 31 he had published the *Minstrelsy of the Borders*, a two-volume collection of ballads, many previously unpublished.

The book was a success. Scott continued writing in the manly form of poetry; 'The Lay of the Last Minstrel' was an instant best-seller.

He produced a series of epic poems; 'Marmion' featuring the build-up to the battle of Flodden, 'The Lady of the Lake', about the conflict between James V and the Douglases, and 'Lord of the Isles', culminating in the Battle of Bannockburn. Scottish history was being exposed in a new accessible, romantic style – and the reading public loved it.

In 1814 Scott took an outrageous step and published in a (fairly) new modern media – the novel! Novels were regarded pretty much as 'pulp fiction'; even women were writing them. The stigma was

Walter Scott.

such that Scott published anonymously. When *Waverly* was a success, subsequent novels were designated as 'by the author of Waverly'.

He had invented the 'historical novel', where fictional characters mingle with real historical persons to tell an entertaining version of the past.

If the style of *Waverly* was controversial, the content was incendiary. The book's alternative title was *Tis Sixty Years Since*. It was about a young Englishman's adventures in the Jacobite '45 rising and treats the 'rebels' (and even the Highlanders) with some respect. In polite society treating the 'rebellion' as anything other than a scurrilous plot and treating the clans as anything other than 'thieving Catholic Highland bastards' had been unthinkable. The public loved it.

The king's visit

By the time the king's visit came around Walter Scott was a highly respected writer and a vibrant modern reinterpreter of Scottish history. He had been knighted by Prince George himself. He was a literary superstar. He was 'The Wizard of the North'. Who better to stage manage a royal Scottish extravaganza?

The object was to celebrate George IV's Scottish heritage. It would present him as a JACOBITE king, no less. He was, after all, the great, great, great, great grandson of James VI. He was the descendent of Robert the Bruce, Malcolm Canmore and Kenneth MacAlpin. He was king of Scots; why should he not parade his 'Scottishness'?

The truly bizarre thing about the affair was that the style adopted was HIGHLAND. Highland and Islanders had been on the periphery of Scottish politics since the MacAlpins retreated east out of Dal Riata. Much of it had for centuries been under foreign (Scandinavian) rule and even after it was officially Scottish it maintained an entirely separate cultural trajectory.

For many civilised people in Edinburgh their impression of Highlanders would have been as rebels or beggars.

But from a theatrical point of view Highland costume was a gift. Mainstream Scottish costume had varied little from the English for centuries: Highland dress was a whole new ball gown!

The king was kitted out with a splendid facsimile of imagined Highland ensemble. The whole thing assembled from (what is now called) Royal Stuart tartan, although he did wear pink stockings to hide his peely-wally legs.

Highland chieftains were invited, although some were appalled by the liberties being taken with their traditions. Scott published a booklet, *HINTS addressed to the INHABITANTS OF EDINBURGH AND OTHERS in prospect of HIS MAJESTY'S VISIT*, so the public would be informed of the new etiquette.

Most startling was that all the Scottish nobles invited to the 'Grand Highland Ball' were informed that … 'no Gentleman is to be allowed to appear in anything but the ancient Highland costume'. Having to don this primitive fancy dress must have felt like a calculated insult, but the king was not to be disappointed. There was a mad scramble for any scraps of tartanish materials with which to mock up costumes.

George cartoon.

TARTAN

It turned out that tartan was not just for the king's visit – it stuck. While the Highlands continued to be devastated by clearances, 'Balmoralisation' – ersatz versions of Gaelic dress and custom – were suddenly mainstream.

Feudal lords (many of Norman descent) found their families being referred to as 'clans'.

Textiles with a chequered pattern appear in Celtic culture as far back as eight centuries before Christ. In Medieval Scotland patterns we would recognise as tartan became popular among the clans of the Highlands and Islands.

There was no particular ownership of a pattern by any clan or family. However, the number of weavers in an area would be small. Setting up a new pattern is complicated, so a weaver would repeat the same design over and over. The result was that many people in the same area would wear similar fabric.

> BY THE WAY: A PLAID is a square of fabric worn as a kilt or a shawl, WHETHER OR NOT it has a tartan pattern on it!

After 1822 every noble family was expected to have its own unique tartan. This was then formalised by two English chancers, John and Charles Allen. Calling themselves the Sobieski Stuarts, they claimed to be grandsons of Bonny Prince Charlie (Charlie's mother was a Sobieski). They wrote two books in the 1840s documenting an entirely fictitious ancient history of the clan tartans.

Tartan patterns are part of Highland culture, but the whole mythology of sacred ownership of tartans by clans and families is a nineteenth-century invention. And Walter Scott is the man to blame.

Walter Scott would complete his baronial mansion of Abbotsford (near Galashiels) and fill it with all manner of real and fake Scottish historical memorabilia.

BY THE WAY: Scottish actor Alan Cummings' first reaction to the contents of Abbotsford was *'OOH CAMPORAMA!'*.

He would also become bankrupt when his publishing business collapsed. He tried to write his way out of the crisis but still died penniless. He had made a fortune and lost it.

How do you judge Walter Scott?

This is not an easy question to answer. On the one hand, he most certainly did invent a romantic version of Scotland and its past; the results of which are highly visible, not just on the Royal Mile in Edinburgh, but in the perception of Scotland across the world.

On the other he created an image of Scotland that is deeply flawed and bears very little resemblance to anything approaching actual history.

On the one hand, historian John Keay wrote ...

By concentrating on the historical experience, by examining its institutions, and using its language, he created that consciousness of Scotland which has sustained a sense of nationhood in a country without statehood.

On the other hand, American author Mark Twain wrote ...

with the sillinesses and emptinesses, sham grandeurs, sham gauds, and sham chivalries of a brainless and worthless long-vanished society. He did measureless harm; more real and lasting harm, perhaps, than any other individual that ever wrote.

He certainly has been remembered. The Scott Monument rises 200ft above Princes Street — it is on the border between Edinburgh's Old and New Towns. It couldn't be more central in the nation's capital.

And it is a monument to a writer of pulp fiction.

HIGHLAND PERCEPTION

For centuries the Highlands had been regarded as remote, uncomfortable and peripheral to Scotland. The Highlanders were barbarians. In the eighteenth and nineteenth centuries their entire social structures were destroyed and atrocities were heaped on generations of men, women and children.

But now a version of their culture is dominant in the world's perception of Scotland. If you type 'Scotland' into an online image search, over 50 per cent of the pictures are of the Highlands or are Highland related. If you type 'Scottish people', the largest grouping is of folk wearing tartan in some form or other. The year 1822 is a pretty important one!

FINAL
THOUGHTS

We are a mongrel nation! A 'TRUE SCOT' might be descended from a Mesolithic hunter or a Neolithic farmer, might be descended from Bretonic or Gaelic Celtic culture, might have Irish or Anglo-Saxon forebears. If you'll accept a thousand years or so as being enough time to count you as no longer being 'an incomer', you may have Scandinavian blood either directly from Norway or from Denmark via France in the form of the Normans.

Since the eighteenth century we have had wave after wave of new arrivals from many parts of the globe, each enriching our culture in their own way.

Scotland has always been a divided nation. It was founded by Scots merging with Picts and incorporating south of Scotland Britons. Much later the Gaelic and Norse traditions of the Highlands, Western Isles and Northern Isles were brought under the banner.

Much of the time we have battled each other. Many expect the long-time rivalry with the 'Auld Enemy' to the south to be the major source of conflict, but Scots (of some loyalty) fighting Scots (of some other) has been far more lethal.

And Scotland is still divided. In the early twenty-first century the issue of Scottish independence is very live. The country is split (among voters) at around about fifty-fifty, swinging a few points in either direction. Under democratic rules a single point in a referendum can swing the fate of the nation.

Yet for all that, there is an overwhelming notion of Scottishness and there is a pride in Scotland: a pride in our industrial, techno-logical, scientific and philosophical achievements, a pride in our sportsmen and women and a pride expressed in literature, music, and art.

Across the world there are many who choose to embrace their Scottish roots (no matter how remote) and celebrate their connections with this small land.

The authors hope that this romp through Scotland's past will help some gain a flavour of the journey the country has taken from warring tribes to the unique proud nation of today.